Tasting the
Goodness of God

Tasting the Goodness of God

---

31 Daily Devotionals for Everyday Living

MCKADE MARSHALL

 MLM Publishing

MLM Publishing
PO Box 533
Malibu, California 90265

www.mckademarshall.com

Printed in the United States of America

ISBN 978-0-578-14638-6

Library of Congress Control Number: 2 0 1 4 9 1 3 9 5 2

No endeavor like the writing of this book is ever accomplished without the empowering of the Holy Spirit and the undergirding of intercessory prayer voiced on my behalf by many friends and family members whom I love dearly. From the depths of my heart, thank you.

Contents

PART FOUR
GOD IS ALWAYS FAITHFUL!

PART FIVE
GOD IS ALWAYS YOUR FATHER!

Introduction

For many years I have wanted to write a book. The inspiration to write this book came while I sat listening to a friend play one of the melodies to his newly written musical on the piano. As I was sipping away at my coffee and absorbing my friend's inspirational song, I suddenly felt a stirring within my heart to start writing this book. Writing a book was something I had always started to do in the past, but this time I was starting with much greater resolve.

I knew the time was now.

I walked out of the living room, my friend still hammering away at a new song, and sat down at my desk and began to type. I had no idea where to start on writing a book. I didn't know what to talk about. Life is so multi-dimensional, and my experiences from travels, college, and meeting so many marvelous people along the way were so broad. However, life has not always been an easy road for me. In 2009, the way of life in America seemed to have permanently changed with the economy souring, and so many lives were turned upside down. Several years later some things have seemed to smooth out, but many people are still struggling. I decided my first book must be one full of encouragement. As I sat still, waiting on what I felt in my heart to write, my mind began to flood with encouraging thoughts that *God is always good.* The verse "O taste and see that the LORD is good" from Psalm 34:8 (NASB) ran through my mind like the chorus of a song. On this one Biblical truth I decided to base the premise of this new book.

Many of us shy away from coming to God, not because we dislike or don't trust Him, but because we don't know for sure that He is always good! If God is good all the time, then we can have confidence at all times that trusting Him results in our benefit. Growing up in the Bible Belt of the United States, I frequently heard the expression "God is not like Santa Claus".... but I beg to differ, He is even *better* than Santa Claus. God says to come to Him for *all your needs* and to give Him *all your desires*, not because He does not know them already, but because He wants you to trust Him to meet all your needs and fulfill your desires as you actively pursue Him!

God always has your best interest at heart.

Psalm 16:11 (NASB) says, "You will make known to me the path of life; In Your presence is fullness of joy; In Your right hand there are pleasures forever." The Lord wants to give you direction for the best life possible, fill you with His joy, and give you pleasures forever that are from Him! You may be thinking at this point, "Well, McKade, now you're just tickling our ears like the Apostle Timothy warned! Did God really say that?!" Believe it or not, I looked up these verses myself, and indeed, they are in the Word of God.

God's Word never fails nor can He tell a lie. He is our faithful Creator. Every day we should trust Him to meet our needs and take us to a higher level in our walks with Him. Jesus says in Luke 9:23 that you must deny yourself and come after Him *daily* in order to fulfill your God-given destiny. That means you should be feeding yourself the promises of God *daily*, you should pray to Him *daily*, and you should seek His will *daily*.

When you seek God daily, your life will begin to be filled with the things of God.

James 1:17 (ESV) says, "Every good gift and every perfect gift is from above, coming down from the Father of lights with whom there is no variation or shadow due to change." When you seek God daily, He promises that every good thing out of Heaven is going to start pouring into your life! The peace you need for a situation that is out of control is going to start pouring down. The joy you need to fill any pain in your life is going to fill your heart. The unconditional love you need to reach a loved one or a difficult child is going to flood your life.

With that said, it is very important to seek God every day, so I've organized *Tasting the Goodness of God* into 31 daily devotionals, one devotional for everyday of the month. You can read each devotional in five minutes or less. The devotionals are divided into five different sections. Each section is a declaration about who God is so you can meditate on a different attribute about Him every week. The sections include: *God Is Always Good!*, *God Is Always For You!*, *God Is Always Love!*, *God Is Always Faithful!*, and *God Is Always Your Father!*.

Throughout *Tasting the Goodness of God* I will continually go back to the Scriptures. I believe God has told all of us who He is in the Bible by preserving His words spoken and documented through people moved by His Spirit. To get the most out of each devotional, feel free to follow along by reading Bible verse references on your iPhone "Bible" apps, online search engines, or good old fashioned leather-bound Bibles.

You can either read one devotional a day for an entire
month, or you can read six devotionals a week, taking off
on Sunday, in order to cover each section one week at a
time (with an extra day on the fifth week). I encourage you
to do these devotionals each day with a friend, family
member, or in a small group, as you will likely get more
out of this book by sharing thoughts with other people
seeking God with you.

Each day is titled by one word, followed by a Bible verse
pertaining to that word. I chose one word titles for each
day so that the one word might stick in your mind like a
buzzword you hear on a TV or radio commercial. For
instance, Day 9's "buzzword" is BLESS, so throughout the
day when you think of the word BLESS you will hear the
Scripture of the day, "The Lord will command the blessing
on me..." throughout your day.

At the end of each devotional are the *daily readings* from
the Bible. These readings are usually about 10 verses from
the Old Testament and 10 verses from the New Testament,
and pertain to the devotional just read. I have chosen these
daily readings from all over the Bible in order to give you
a taste of the Scriptures all the way through.

The daily reading is followed by a *thought for the day*.
Thought for the day is a couple of questions regarding the
daily devotional that is designed to stimulate thinking
about what you have read as you go about your day. There
are no right or wrong answers to these questions! These
questions will challenge and encourage you to put to
action what you have just read. When you put God's word
into action that is when you really see God begin to fulfill
His promises in your life!

Introduction

My prayer is that you not only would be encouraged, but also set free from things that are holding you back from God's best in life, while reading *Tasting the Goodness of God*. God is your unchanging, unconditionally loving Father! I pray you experience more healing, more inspiration, and more understanding of God's goodness as you read and put into practice each day's message.

So, here goes. Be blessed!

Part One

God Is Always Good!

Day 1 - *Believe*

**"O taste and see that the Lord is good;
How blessed is the man who takes refuge in Him!"
Psalm 34:8 (NASB)**

I have always believed that God is good. I was just sort of born that way. I knew there was an all-powerful, all-loving "Big Man" in the sky who loved me. It could be because I was born to two parents who loved God, but I believe that notion is sort of just given to all of us when we are born. With small children you do not have to convince them that God is good, as they already know this intuitively. However, as we grow older, life happens. Struggles come. We don't get everything we want. Our neighbor has more, and we don't understand why God didn't give us more; or maybe, we unexplainably lose a loved one.

That's when we come to terms with faith.

Faith requires believing even though life isn't always fair. Times become difficult. The financial pressure rises, the wayward family member gets worse, or our health begins to fail. These are times when what we truly believe in our core comes out. When these tough times come, the best question we can ask ourselves is: "Is God truly who He says He is?" And if so, what does that mean for us?

To understand who God is and who He says He is, we must dive into His Scriptures. John 1:1-3 (NASB) tells us who God is: "In the beginning was the Word, and the

Word was with God, and the Word was God. He was in
the beginning with God. All things came into being
through Him, and apart from Him nothing came into
being that has come into being." So we know that God is
the Word, and all things came into existence through God
and through His Word.

Where can we find God and His Word? By reading and
understanding what the Bible says. All things written in
the Bible were intended to be read and hopefully
understood by all of mankind in order to know and
understand who our God says He is and what that makes
us: His children made in His image and the masterpiece of
His magnificent creation.

In moments of distress, which I tend to frequently have
(being the most dramatic child of all my siblings!), there is
always one thing I know I can do when all else fails. I can
go to God's Word and know that He is always there. I love
the Bible because it is something tangible that represents
Almighty God. All of His flawless words are bound into
one holy book called The Bible.

The Bible will never fail you.

The more you read the Bible, the more your faith grows.
The more your faith grows, the more obstacles you will
overcome and see God's love spring forth in your life! The
Bible is filled with God's great promises for every
believer's life!

2 Peter 1:4 (NASB) states that "He has granted to us His
precious and magnificent promises" and "for as many as
are the promises of God, in Him they are yes" in 2
Corinthians 1:20 (NASB). What are all these precious,
magnificent promises Peter talks about? And how is God's

answer always "yes" when we believe His promises according to Paul? These promises are things God has promised to those who love Him and are saturated throughout the Bible from beginning to end.

From Genesis to Revelation, there are sixty-six books within the Bible. The Bible is divided into to two major sections, the Old Testament (also known as the Old Covenant) and the New Testament (known as the New Covenant). Some of the books are in the form of a letter; others are a recount of ancient Jewish history or oracles passed down from one generation of Jewish people to the next.

The thirty-nine books from the Old Testament include many of the ancient stories of the Jewish people, from the Creation story in Genesis to the prophetic utterances of all the minor and major prophets prophesying during Israel's time as a kingdom established by God, and the ensuing exile to Babylon and return home before Jesus the Messiah was born.

The twenty-seven books from the New Testament retell the stories of Jesus Christ from eyewitness accounts, His teachings, and the apostles' letters to the early Church. The New Testament testifies to the fulfillment of the coming Messiah (translated "Christ") through Jesus, who is the Son of God.

Through these sixty-six books we begin to learn and understand the character of God, who He is, and what He really thinks about us. Once we begin to see the big picture of who God is, we can walk through life at all times knowing God is always good!

GOD IS ALWAYS GOOD!

Daily Reading:
Psalm 34:1-10
Mark 10:17-27

Thought for the Day:
Do I truly believe that God is always good? If so, what does God's will mean for my life? What does that mean for the lives of my spouse, my children, my co-workers, or my parents?

Day 2 - *Know*

**"Be still, and know that I am God; I will be exalted
among the nations, I will be exalted in the earth!"
Psalm 46:10 (NKJV)**

"Let go!" "Relax!" "Give up worrying." How
often we need to hear those words! Yet God continually
tells us throughout the Scriptures these very things. With
an average 70,000 thoughts soaring through our minds
every day (and even more on a busy day!), our minds are
cluttered with the things of the world around us.

*Of those myriad of thoughts, 90% of them are of yesterday and
repeat today.*

Imagine for a moment if you could standing outside of
your brain and look into your head like you were peering
into a fish bowl and there were 70,000 "fish", or thoughts,
swarming around in there. It would look like utter chaos!
Then, consider that there were only two kinds of fish. One
fish is good, or what we call good thoughts. Another fish is
bad, or bad thoughts. Which "fish" would you choose to
catch to look at in each of these brief moments?

God tells us in His Word which thoughts, or as I used in
the example "fish", to catch and observe. Philippians 4:8
(NIV) says, "Finally, brothers and sisters, whatever is true,
whatever is noble, whatever is right, whatever is pure,
whatever is lovely, whatever is admirable--if anything is
excellent or praiseworthy--*think about such things.*"

GOD IS ALWAYS GOOD!

Today, many of us go around thinking and entertaining all sorts of negative thoughts when we're not careful. Some thoughts are provoked by things outside our control. Work was rough so all your complaints run rampant through your mind. Your family is fighting again and all your thoughts tell you your home is falling apart and isn't going to make it. That colleague made more cutting remarks today and you're ready to fire back. But God has a different answer. God tells us:

You have the power to rule over your thoughts.

Instead of always thinking of the worst, you know God is who He says He is and that He repays evil with good. Work was difficult, but you know that promotion or something even better is coming so you work harder as if you were working to the Lord. Your family is fighting but you know God is the author of peace, and not confusion, so you stand on God's Word that He will bring peace to every family situation. That colleague just made a cutting remark, but you know God says to repay evil with good so you downplay the comment and take the higher road knowing you are a child of the Most High God.

God even tells us in Proverbs 23:7 (NASB), "For as a man thinks within himself, so he is." If 90% of the same positive thoughts ran through our minds every day, how drastically would that change our lives! Instead of growing bitter towards life, you find life growing better and better every day. Instead of walking around sour without hope, you know God already has solutions and promises of blessings on the way.

The more we set our thoughts on who God says He is and His promises, the more we will see our minds grow toward the great things God has in store for us. He even promises in Proverbs 4:18 that every day our lives will grow "brighter and brighter" until we reach our full destiny.

The next time that negative thought comes, you can ignore that thought. Reach for a new thought: a good thought, a praiseworthy report, an excellent idea, a noble plan. Put on the mind of Christ, knowing that God's plans for you are always good and expect God's best is on its way!

Daily Reading:
Psalm 46:1-11
Philippians 4:1-9

Thought for the Day:
Is there an area of strife in your life? What areas of your life do you need to hand over to God that are beyond your control? What areas of life do you need to change your thinking toward?

Day 3 - *Understand*

"Don't act thoughtlessly, but understand what the Lord
wants you to do."
Ephesians 5:17 (NLT)

T hroughout God's Word the writers often refer to
God's will. Jesus even goes as far to say in Matthew 7:21
(NLT), "Not everyone who calls out to me, 'Lord! Lord!'
will enter the Kingdom of Heaven. Only those who
actually *do the will of my Father in heaven* will enter." So
what is the Lord's will for each of our lives?

One of the most profound statements summarizing the
Lord's will is found in a prayer most of us have likely
heard many times: The Lord's Prayer. Jesus begins His
model prayer with His disciples in Matthew 6:9-10 (NKJV)
praying, "Our Father in heaven, Hallowed be Your name.
Your kingdom come. Your will be done On earth as it is in
heaven." Jesus states that God's will is the same on earth
as it is in Heaven. In other words:

*God's will is to bring the realities of Heaven where He is to the
realities of earth where you are.*

What exists in Heaven? Love, joy, peace, life, abundance,
healing, restoration, and the Father Himself. So we see
God's will is to bring love, joy, peace, life, abundance,
healing, restoration and even His Spirit to dwell within us!
As we walk with God daily, our lives become a reflection
of what is going on in Heaven. We carry the life of God

11

within us. As Jesus says in Matthew 17:21, "the kingdom of God is within you".

The best model for God's will in our lives is by looking at the life of Jesus and imitating His example while He walked on the earth. Elements of Jesus' life on earth consisted of frequent prayer, teaching of the Scriptures, and loving each person He encountered. Fulfilling God's will is actually much simpler than our intellect might think.

The starting place to entering God's kingdom is from the eyes of a child.

Jesus drives home the point of child-like faith when He says in Matthew 18:3 (NIV), "Truly I tell you, unless you change and become like little children, you will never enter the kingdom of heaven." How do we become like children pertaining to the things of God?

First, we must understand the attributes of a child and apply them to our faith even in adulthood. Think back to your childhood. When you were born, you didn't ask your parents to feed you. You simply knew you were hungry and your parents fed you. Not only did your parents feed you, they clothed you, comforted you, trained you, and encouraged you as you grew. As you grew older, you began to feed yourself, clothe yourself, and grow to full maturity.

In our spiritual journey, the same can be applied. The Scriptures refer to our spiritual journey beginning by first being "born again" by accepting Christ to come live in our hearts. Spiritually speaking, you did not birth yourself nor fed yourself the things of God before you came to know Christ. But as we begin to grow in the things of God, we read the Bible, we pray, and seek God in our lives, we begin to grow spiritually until we grow spiritually mature. This is the will of God for each of our lives.

God's will for your life is for you to grow to full spiritual maturity.

Paul puts it this way in Philippians 3:14 (NLT), "I press on to reach the end of the race". The will of God is for us to run toward the things of God throughout our lives. As we make decisions daily, with God's help, our lives begin to look more like Christ's life and our spirits grow so that we know God more.

The more spiritually mature we become, the more real heaven becomes as we see God at work in our lives. Always remember that as God's child His kingdom, or heaven, is always inside of you ready to come out!

Daily Reading:
Micah 6:1-8
Ephesians 5:8-21

Thought for the Day:
Where do you need more of God's kingdom and the things of God in your life? Is there an area you need to ask God for healing, grace, restoration, or something else that only God can give?

Day 4 - *Hope*

"Hope deferred makes the heart sick, but a longing
fulfilled is a tree of life."
Proverbs 13:12 (NIV)

My first experience with hope that I can recall was
when I was a little boy. Every few weeks my father would
take me to the local toy store and allow me to pick out one
new toy. Often my dad would tell me in advance that he
was getting me a toy but usually it wasn't that day. While I
was disappointed that I didn't get a toy right then, I was
still excited and hopeful Dad would deliver on his
promise.

Then a week or so would come around, and Dad would
tell me it was time to go to the toy store. I could hardly
wait for those weekends! I was so ecstatic on the car ride
from the house to the toy store I would be in a trance of
delight daydreaming about the possibilities of which new
toy would now join my collection. After waiting for days
(and what seemed like years to a young child!) I knew my
hope of receiving that new toy was about to be fulfilled
and life was good!

Every time we visited the store I picked out the exact toy I
wanted. If it was a toy car, I wanted it to be red with a
remote control to navigate it, and it had to be the fastest
car in the store. If it was a dinosaur, it had to look like a
real one, be the same size as all my other dinosaurs, and
couldn't talk or sing like Barney! For a little kid, I was
quite particular.

GOD IS ALWAYS GOOD!

Every time I received exactly what I was asking for.

Jesus shares a similar idea of what hope is and what to expect in the fulfillment of hope by asking our Father in Heaven through prayer. He says in Matthew 7:11 (NASB), "If you then, being evil, know how to give good gifts to your children, how much more will your Father who is in heaven give what is good to those who ask Him!" When we put our hope in God, the fulfillment of hope or the gift we receive is always going to be good.

How often do we go through life not asking God exactly what we are looking for because we are afraid He will respond with something we don't want to hear or don't trust is good from our perspective? God wants us to put our hope in Him for what we are asking and *expect* that what He has for us is always good!

God is the Creator of the universe and all mankind. He knows you better than you know you. He knows what you prefer even more than you know what you know you prefer because *He made you.* So when you come to your Father in heaven you can know with absolute confidence that His response to your request is always good!

Sometimes you do not have because you do not ask.

In the Scriptures, James 4:2 tells us that sometimes we are lacking in a certain area of life simply because we have not asked yet! Are you feeling tired or run down all the time? Do ends seem to not meet lately? Is your marriage struggling?

I encourage you to tell God what it is you need. Place your hope in Him to be your source in all things. Remind Him of His promises. Father, you said you would renew my strength because I hope in you (Isaiah 40:31). God, you said I would be the head and not the tail (Deuteronomy 28:13). Lord, you said whom God has joined together in marriage let no man separate (Mark 10:9).

How many promises of God are we placing our hope in for Him to fulfill? All throughout the Bible God continually encourages His children to look to Him for everything they need in life and even admonishes them when they don't. The principle still holds true today. Trust God and know that, like a good parent, His response to our needs and requests are always good!

Daily Reading:
Proverbs 13:12-22
Matthew 7:1-12

Thought for the Day:
Do you believe that God's responses to your prayers are always good? If so, when things aren't happening as fast as you would like or you don't find the answer you are looking for, are you willing to hope in Him and wait expectantly? What are some specific things you desire from God and should be asking of Him?

Day 5 - *Trust*

**"Whoever can be trusted with very little can also be
trusted with much."
Luke 16:10 (NIV)**

T rust is the confident expectation of something or
someone. If your boss tells you, "I am giving you more
responsibilities than your colleagues because I *trust* you,"
then it is probably because your boss knows he can count
on you every time to get the job done right.

Being trustworthy is something we should all strive
toward. Whether we are at work, at school, with our
families at home, or anywhere we go we are continually
either building up trust or losing trust. When we make a
conscious effort every day to do what's right then we
begin to build trust with all people in our lives.

God desires you to be trustworthy.

In your walk with God the more people learn you are
someone who can be counted on, they not only begin to
trust what you can do for them but also what they can do
for you. In the example of a boss bestowing more
responsibility on a trustworthy employee, the boss is
enabled to give the employee a raise or a promotion.

Many times we ask God for a raise or for a promotion in
life, but sometimes we first need to examine ourselves. Are
you someone who can be counted on? Are you faithful day

in and day out? Whether you make much money or little money is irrelevant to the Lord when it comes to being counted as trustworthy.

In the book of Matthew Jesus tells a parable of three men who are given a task by their master before he returns from his journey. The first servant is given five talents, the second servant two talents and the last receives only one talent. The first two servants double their talents but the last servant hides his talent while the master is gone. When the master returns he blesses and rewards his first two servants for multiplying their talents, while the third he rebukes sharply and takes away what little he has.

In God's kingdom the Lord has given each of us talents while here on the earth. Some of us are given the ability to speak well, others the ability to nurture people back to health, while others have a heart to serve the next generation. There are many talents God has given us. Are you being faithful with the talents God has already given you?

When you are faithful with what you have right now, God will give you even more.

The Lord longs to give us more in this life! God gives to those who are counted trustworthy. For some of us, we doubt ourselves and God gives us even more to show us that we have what it takes. We are trustworthy in God's eyes.

Did you know that the instant you accepted Jesus into your heart, God instantly deemed you 100% trustworthy to build His kingdom? What a blessing and a privilege we have in this life! God has called us blessed so that we can bless others. God has called us free from sin so we can free others. God has called us alive in His Spirit so we can bring life and healing to others.

I believe even right now that God is pouring out more on your life because He sees you as trustworthy. You are a child of God Most High and highly favored! You already have much because His Son Jesus poured out His life so that you could live an abundant life full of talents!

Daily Reading:
Proverbs 3:1-12
Matthew 25:14-30

Thought for the Day:
What talents has the Lord already given you? How can you multiply those talents in your service to the Lord and those around you? What people in your life already have talents that you can encourage them in?

Day 6 - *Love*

**"For God loved the world so much that He gave His one
and only Son, so that everyone who believes in Him will
not perish but have eternal life."
John 3:16 (NLT)**

The pinnacle of God's love for us was in giving His
Son Jesus Christ to die for our sins on the Cross then
raising Him up to eternal life so that we might be forgiven
in God's eyes and inherit eternal life with Him forever.
What a marvelous act and promise from God!

Love is the very theme of the entire Bible and God's
message to mankind. Paul describes love in 1 Corinthians
13 as being patient, kind, keeping no account of
wrongdoings, never failing and other attributes.
Throughout the Word of God everything hinges on this
one thing.

God loves you. The love of God will never fail you.

The apostle John even says in 1 John 4:18 that love is so
powerful that it can cast out your greatest fears. What fears
are you holding on to that God wants you to cast aside so
He can fill it with His love?

Growing up I always feared I would never measure up to
what God has called me to in this life. I feared I would
never reach my destiny. What I was forgetting is that God
promises on our journey with Him through this life that
He will never leave us nor forsake us (Deuteronomy 31:6).

GOD IS ALWAYS GOOD!

As I've grown older, I realize it is not me who will get me to my destiny but God and His love working through me.

In order to fulfill our destinies in this world we must first be able to receive the love of God so that we can freely give it away. 1 John 4:7 (NKJV) says, "Beloved, let us love one another, for love is of God; and everyone who loves is born of God and knows God."

The more you know the love of God, the more you know how to love others.

The apostle James describes loving our neighbors as being the royal law fulfilling all of Scripture (James 2:8). If we know that God is patient, kind, and generous toward us then we know how to be patient, kind, and generous toward others. How can you grow in the love of God?

You grow in the love of God by loving others.

By putting others before yourself in love you are fulfilling the royal law of Scripture. A small act of kindness can change a person's day.

Your love grows for others by small acts of kindness every day.

You smile and tell the cashier at the grocery store to have a great day, making that worker's day a little brighter. You listen to a friend who had a hard day after you just got off from a long day at work. You serve at a soup kitchen every month to help the hungry and less fortunate in your neighborhood. All these small acts of kindness demonstrate the love of God.

The most difficult form of love is loving our enemies. Jesus commands that we pray for and bless our enemies. He says in Matthew 5:43-44 (NASB), "You have heard that it was said, 'You shall love your neighbor and hate your enemy.' But I say to you, love your enemies and pray for those who persecute you." Again, Jesus tells us in Luke 6:35 (NASB), "But love your enemies, and do good, and lend, expecting nothing in return; and your reward will be great, and you will be sons of the Most High; for He Himself is kind to ungrateful and evil men."

If God's kindness pours out over people who do not love Him, how much more should we show love toward those who are against us! As we show love toward our enemies, praying for them and acting kindly toward them, not only do we store up rewards from God in heaven, but we also allow God to change their hearts.

Our life motto should be: "Love God. Love people." This is the fulfillment of all God's laws!

Daily Reading:
Song of Solomon 8:1-7
1 Corinthians 13:1-13

Thought for the Day:
How many people have you told this week that God loves them? What are different small acts of kindness you can show people you see every day to fulfill the royal law of loving your neighbor?

Part Two

God Is Always For You!

Day 7 - *Conquer*

**"In all these things we are more than conquerors
through Him who loved us."
Romans 8:37 (NIV)**

In the Old Testament a man of God named Joshua was deemed with the task of conquering a land full of people who did not serve God so Israel could settle the promised land from God after leaving Egypt and the wilderness. Now Joshua was different from all the other leaders in the history of Israel. Joshua always followed exactly what God told him to do without fail, trusting in God, and he successfully led an entire tribe of young men, women, and children into the Promised Land.

God promised to go before Israel and drive out their enemies before them. The enemies before Israel were much greater and more established. Israel was a small tribe, weary from dwelling forty years in the desert. It would take an act of God for Israel to inherit the Promised Land!

All God was asking Israel to do is believe Him and obey what He said to do, and He would give them swift victory. When Israel disobeyed and rebelled against God's command, things went awry. Then Israel would inevitably recommit their hearts to God, and He would forgive them and move on their behalf.

In Luke 10:19 Jesus tells us that we have been given authority over *all* the power of the enemy. In our own lives, when we stay close to God, like Joshua, we are always guaranteed God will go before us and give us success. We cannot be defeated when we are in Him!

You have victory over the enemy every time.

When the enemy comes to remind you of your past, you can ignore him. You have already been given the victory. When the enemy tries to bring fear into your life, you know you cannot fail because God has already gone before you. 2 Samuel 22:40 (NLT) promises, "You have subdued my enemies under my feet"!

When your adversaries come, where do they belong? Under your feet! Isaiah 54:17 (NLT) even says that "no weapon formed against you will succeed". Whatever is against you in this life, God promises that it will not succeed because He is going before you!

God is always for you.

Get that deep inside your spirit. God is always pressing forward and desires to see you overcome and succeed in life. Is there an addiction you are struggling with? God is moving heaven and earth to break that addiction from your life. A problem at work? God already has solutions on the way. A shortage of resources? God is Jehovah-jireh, the Lord our Provider. A bad health report? God is our Healer and Great Physician.

For years after college I struggled with the idea that God really was for me. So many difficult situations had come into my life. Success was not coming as quickly as before. The economy was sluggish. People weren't as optimistic about the future. However, a few close friends told me what I'm telling you.

GOD IS ALWAYS FOR YOU!

You are more than a conqueror.

You were placed where you are today by God in order to overcome and completely conquer all things the enemy brings your way and help others conquer quickly too. Every difficulty is a setup God allows in your life so that you will quickly conquer and make His name great!

God's people should be known as more than conquerors. When the whole world seems against you, you know that the Creator of the universe is already moving things in your favor so that you can quickly conquer!

Daily Reading:
Joshua 1:1-9
Romans 8:31-39

Thought for the Day:
What areas of life do you feel defeated in that you need to declare God's victory over? What are some areas that you can recommit to God so that He can give you swift victory like Joshua and the Israelites in the Promised Land?

Day 8 - *Overcome*

**"And they overcame him because of the blood of the
Lamb and because of the word of their testimony."
Revelation 12:11 (NASB)**

O ne of the best ways to overcome different
situations and hardships we go through in life is by
hearing the stories of others. These stories about people
overcoming are called "testimonies" in the Scriptures. The
more we share our stories with others, the more others feel
empowered to overcome similar situations in life.

*It is important to share your stories of overcoming in life with
other people.*

When you share your story, you are helping others get
through difficult situations you have lived through. Many
times people who are struggling feel like they are the only
one. That's what the enemy wants you to believe. If he can
isolate you then he has cut off your power. However, as
believers we can disarm the enemy by confiding in one
another about our struggles.

In this life there is always going to be battles, obstacles,
opposition, and struggles but every time God promises
you that you will overcome each situation by trusting in
Him. As you look to God as your source He releases
strength, wisdom, understanding, creativity, knowledge,
and everything you need in order to greatly overcome
whatever is standing in front of you.

GOD IS ALWAYS FOR YOU!

The power of your story defeats the enemy every time.

Every time you tell people of what God has done in your life, you are trampling over the enemy. By speaking the word of your testimony, or your story, you are releasing faith both over yourself and over those listening. The enemy cannot trump faith!

Faith is the currency of heaven and the ingredient God requires in order to operate on our behalf. Hebrews 11:6 (NLT) says, "And it is impossible to please God without faith. Anyone who wants to come to Him must believe that God exists and that He rewards those who sincerely seek Him." When you operate in faith, believe God is who He says He is, then God must do what He says He will do!

Your faith is your testimony.

No matter where you are in your journey with God, whether you have just begun walking with God or you have walk with God many years, your testimony is already written in God's book in Heaven. The psalmist David says in Psalm 139:16 (NLT), "You saw me before I was born. Every day of my life was recorded in your book. Every moment was laid out before a single day had passed." In other words, God already knows what's in your future, and your future is you overcame. What a magnificent promise we have from God! You are already destined to succeed!

Since we know according to God's Word we have already overcome every struggle, every opposition, and every battle that comes our way, we can confidently stand in times of trouble knowing these things are quickly passing. The more we look to God and trust His Word, the greater our testimony is when we pass each test we go through in life.

God never promised us we would never have trouble or heartache in this life, but He did promise that we would more than overcome everything that comes our way because He has already seen our future and our future is blessed!

Daily Reading:
Psalm 139:13-24
Revelation 12:1-11

Thought for the Day:
What is a story about overcoming in your life that you are ready to share with others? What is a trial you are going through right now that you need to put your trust in God in order to deliver you through?

Day 9 - *Bless*

"The LORD will command the blessing on you in your barns and in all that you undertake. And He will bless you in the land that the LORD your God is giving you." Deuteronomy 28:8 (ESV)

One of the greatest hopes we have in God is His promise to always bless us. When we follow God His blessings spill out into all areas of our lives. He blesses us when we go to work. He blesses us when we rest and sleep. He blesses us when we are at the grocery store. He even blesses us when we may not feel blessed and things don't look so great on the outside.

The Bible says in Galatians 3:13-14 that we are blessed because Jesus became the curse for us. All of our shortcomings in life deserving of punishment fell upon God's Son Jesus so that we would be blessed in this life and in the life to come. It may seem unfair but this is the grace of God.

In the Scriptures something very dramatic changed when Jesus Christ came to earth. In the Old Testament, Israel and the Jewish people continually failed to live up to the Law God gave to Moses establishing God's first covenant with mankind, which hindered the blessings of God because of their shortcomings. When Jesus came in the New Testament He established a new and better covenant based upon God's grace and not upon the Law.

GOD IS ALWAYS FOR YOU!

As followers of Christ we have been transferred from the Old Covenant of God's Law in the Old Testament to the New Covenant of God's Grace in the New Testament. Under this new covenant, we are perpetually called blessed because we believe in Jesus Christ, Whom God sent to make us right in His eyes forever by washing away our sins in Jesus' blood. As believers we are always covered by the blood of Christ, which atones for, or covers, all of our shortcomings in this life.

At all times and under all circumstances, you are always blessed.

God's nature is always to bless because God is always good! As you begin each day, practice commanding the blessing in different areas of your life and the lives of your loved ones.

Speak what you desire to see.

God has placed unique desires in your heart that He fully intends to bless and fulfill, but we first must speak those desires to see them come to fruition. In Matthew 21 Jesus encourages His disciples to speak the blessing. He says our words of faith are so powerful that we can even dislodge a seemingly immovable mountain when we ask in full faith.

If things in your life don't look blessed begin speaking the blessing. My car doesn't always start on the first try, but Father I declare my car is blessed when I leave for work and when I drive home. My finances look like I will never make it, but God I declare my money is blessed and my money will be multiplied in all that I use it for. The doctor says this disease will get the best of me, but Father I command that my body is healed in Jesus' name!

GOD IS ALWAYS FOR YOU!

When you begin to command the blessing God dispatches His angels to go to work on your behalf. The powers of darkness are broken and God begins to shine His light of healing, of restoration, of peace, of provision, and of all that you need for the breakthrough. As you command the blessing, God commands His blessings over you!

Daily reading:
Deuteronomy 28:1-14
Galatians 3:10-18

Thought for the Day:
What are some areas of your life you need to start commanding the blessing over? What are some of the desires God has placed in your heart that you need to begin speaking outloud?

Day 10 - *Favor*

**"For You, O Lord, will bless the righteous;
With favor You will surround him as with a shield."
Psalm 5:12 (NKJV)**

In the unseen spiritual realm there is a massive war going on that our human eyes cannot see. At times we may sense deep within or through a set of circumstances the effects of what is happening in the unseen spiritual realm. As we seek God, turning away from the power of sin in our lives, and choose to do what is right by God's standards, we begin walking in what the Bible calls God's favor. We are shielded from the power of dark forces that we cannot always see.

In the dictionary, favor is defined as "excessive kindness", "unfair partiality", or "preferential treatment". God bestows favor on those who walk after Him because He knows they will fulfill His desires here on the earth. The book of Genesis tells of a time when all of mankind had turned away from God, except for one man named Noah. Genesis 6:8 (NIV) tell us, "Noah found favor in the eyes of the Lord."

Noah did what was right in God's eyes and God chose to pour out His excessive kindness on Noah and all his family. Because Noah had God's favor, God tells Noah to build an Ark and saves him and his family's life from a global flood that destroys the whole earth. Notice, God shielded Noah from being destroyed by His favor.

GOD IS ALWAYS FOR YOU!

You are shielded from harm by God's favor.

Jesus says in John 10:10 (NASB), "The thief comes only to steal and kill and destroy; I came that they may have life, and have it abundantly." How does God combat the enemy and destroyer in your life? With His favor!

Not only does He protect you from harm, but 1 Peter 5:6 says that at just the right time He will honor you in the eyes of people. Where the enemy intends to harm you, God will turn around and honor you with His favor!

You were created for honor.

God pours out His favor on you so that He can honor you for upholding what He has said to do in His Word. When you are devoted to Him, reading the Word, praying and seeking Him daily, He will always follow through by pouring out His favor in all areas of your life for people to see.

You always have God's favor.

Because you belong to God through Christ, you inherit all the promises God has made throughout the Bible. Wherever you turn, God's favor goes with you. The Lord tells us in Joshua 1:3 that every place you walk God has given to you. In other words, you have victory no matter where you go!

When you have God's favor, people go out of their way to be good to you. You receive promotions, bonuses, and unexpected blessings.

God's favor is one way He expresses His love for you in everyday life.

GOD IS ALWAYS FOR YOU!

As we go about our day and see God's favor at work in our lives, we should always turn to thank Him. A cell phone bill is $20 off this month. Thank You Lord! That cashier discounts your favorite shirt half off. Praise You Father! The neighbor mows your lawn after a heavy rain. God is good!

Thank the Lord every day for His favor. He loves you so much and is always fighting for you!

Daily Reading:
Psalm 5:1-12
John 10:7-18

Thought for the Day:
Where do you have the favor of God in your life, and you need to praise Him for the blessing? What are incidences in your life that you realize you were protected from harm because of God's favor and protection?

Day 11 - *Reach*

**"Brothers and sisters, I know that I have not yet reached
that goal, but there is one thing I always do. Forgetting
the past and straining toward what is ahead."
Philippians 3:13 (NCV)**

O ne of my favorite times of the year is spring. The
winter freezes begin to cease, and the soothing rains of
spring arrive. All the trees, once barren of leaves and fruit,
begin showing signs of new life. Beautiful green leaves and
dormant flowers begin to bud and blossom. A new season
has begun.

Ecclesiastes 3:1 tells us that there is a new season coming
for every activity in our lives. When we go through
hardships and different trials we can always look forward
expectantly knowing that a new season is coming.

A new season is always on its way.

If you are going through a difficult time right now, or
maybe you just came out of a difficult season, know that
better seasons are just around the corner. The Lord
encourages us in Scriptures to always reach forward to
what is coming. He is the God of progress. He is always
moving forward.

Today is the day to reach forward.

My favorite sport in the spring is track and field. Track and field is one of the oldest and most widely participated sports in human history. Dating back to 776 BC in ancient Olympia, Greece, the first track and field games began with men competing in footraces. As the games gained popularity these games granted great fame and glory to the victors.

In Paul's letter to the church in Philippi he encourages his readers to run as an Olympian runs for a prize of great fame and glory. In other words, never stop moving forward in your walk with God. There is always a new level of glory God wants to take you to in your walk with Him.

In our daily walks with God Jesus tells us to never look back. He says in Luke 9:62 (NLT), "Anyone who puts a hand to the plow and then looks back is not fit for the Kingdom of God."

In order to see your future you must stop looking at the past.

The past does not define your future. Every day is a new opportunity to cast a fresh, new vision for your life. Do you have ideas and dreams you have longed to accomplish that God has put in your heart? Release your faith and start to move toward that dream.

Maybe God has placed it in your heart to start a ministry, a new business, a new exercise program or write a book. Take a step of faith today towards your dream. Romans 8:31 says, "If God is for us, who can be against us?" As you begin to take action God is already working on your behalf.

GOD IS ALWAYS FOR YOU!

Taking one small step of faith is one giant step toward seeing your dream come to pass.

 One small step is all God requires to see Him begin pulling the puzzle pieces together for your dream to come to pass. Do you have a dream to have your own ministry? Practice by reaching out to others you encounter each day. To get back in shape? Call that good friend and go for a walk together. To write a book? Pick up the pen and start writing that first page.

If you will do your part to bring your dream to pass then God will do His part and bring all the pieces you will need along the way!

Daily Reading:
Ecclesiastes 3:1-12
Philippians 3:12-21

Thought for the Day:
What dreams has God placed in your heart that you know are from Him? What steps can you take today to see them come to pass?

Day 12 - *Finish*

**"I have fought the good fight, I have finished the race,
I have kept the faith."
2 Timothy 4:7 (NIV)**

Throughout life things don't always go the way we intend it to. A marriage fails. You lose your job. A friend turns their back on you. You get another bad break. The Bible says difficult times and disappointments will come in this life. We live in a fallen world. The key to staying up during these difficult times is to develop a comeback mentality.

You may fall but you always comeback stronger.

When God breathed His life into you He placed His comeback power in you. Romans 8:11 (NIV) says, "He who raised Christ from the dead will also give life to your mortal bodies because of His Spirit who lives in you." Every time life deals you a bad break God's Spirit inside you is taking note and already has a comeback on its way. God even says in Proverbs 6:31 that when the enemy attacks our lives and we suffer loss then he must repay it seven times!

Any time you suffer a wrong in life your Father in Heaven is already calculating your losses for the enemy to repay. One way God repays the enemy is by raising you up stronger than you were before. The Lord will strengthen you to get more done faster than you expected. What used to be difficult to accomplish is now seamless. He will grant you more wisdom, more knowledge, and more understanding as you go through each day.

Your time to comeback is always now.

As you choose to trust God in difficult times you are already walking in your comeback power from whatever you have suffered. As you feed your spirit with God's Word and prayer you are strengthening the Holy Spirit within you to work the impossible in your life.

When impossible situations and difficulties come Paul says in 2 Timothy 1:6 (ESV), "For this reason I remind you to fan into flame the gift of God, which is in you." As you pray and believe God's Word you are giving the gifts God has given you comeback power so that you can finish the race God has set before you in this life.

God has given you His Spirit to ensure you complete your purpose. When you give your heart to the Lord you cannot mess up the plans God has for your life. We all mess up. The key is to trust God when we fall short and get back up.

Your comeback changes your life and the lives of others.

When you have a comeback God uses it to bless you and others in your life. You let go of a past harmful relationship and it frees you up to a healthier, more fulfilling relationship. You lose one job but find a better job with better benefits to provide for your family. Your critical friend walks out on you, but now you have more room in your life for encouraging friends who speak life into your dreams.

God has placed comebacks at different points throughout your life because He wants to display His glory in you!

GOD IS ALWAYS FOR YOU!

The Lord is always fighting for you until you are called home to be with Him in Heaven. God promises in Philippians 1:6 (NKJV) that, "He who has begun a good work in you will complete it."

Each day choose to stay in faith knowing that God has comeback solutions until every area of your life is complete!

Daily Reading:
Proverbs 6:20-31
2 Timothy 4:1-8

Thought for the Day:
What are some of the gifts God has given you that you can fan into flame through prayer and reading His Word? What are some unfinished tasks in your life that God is showing you that you need to use your gifts to complete?

Part Three

God Is Always Love!

Day 13 - *Honor*

**"Be devoted to one another in love. Honor one another
above yourselves."
Romans 12:10 (NIV)**

In Jesus' final days on the earth He said that the world
would know us by the love we have for one another (John
13:35). How we treat the people around us every day at
school, at work, at home, and in public is a reflection of
what is really in our hearts. If we ever find ourselves in the
day being rude, impatient, or quickly offended toward
others then it's time to pause and check what is really
going on in our hearts.

How well you love is a condition of the heart.

Love in action is not always easy. When we love others
what we are really doing is setting aside our own need to
help fulfill the needs of others. This type of love is the crux
of Jesus' message in the Bible.

When you love others you are really loving God.

Putting others before yourself in honor is the greatest form
of love in this world. When our hearts are right with God
our ability to love others comes naturally, like waters
flowing from a fresh wellspring. Jesus tells us in John 7:38
(ESV) that, "Whoever believes in Me, as the Scripture has
said, 'Out of his heart will flow rivers of living water.'"

When you love others your life takes on much greater purpose. Loving others is part of fulfilling your God-given destiny. While God wants to bless you and give you the desires of your heart, He also wants you to love others.

You are God's love to this world.

In 1 Corinthians 12 the apostle Paul describes all followers of Christ as one member of a body with many different body parts. Your gifts vary from the gifts of others who are seeking the Lord. Paul chooses the human body as an example because he is making the point that our bodies, or our lives, are each designed in a unique way to minister as ambassadors of God in this world.

You are God's ambassador.

2 Corinthians 5:20 (NKJV) says, "Now then, we are ambassadors for Christ, as though God were pleading through us: we implore you on Christ's behalf, be reconciled to God." Your purpose in this world is to draw others to God, and really it should be the primary desire of all our hearts because God is love! Only God can ultimately heal the issues in each of our lives.

As an ambassador you represent who God is to those in your life. What a high calling! While this job description can be overwhelming given how awesome and perfect our God is, we can be at peace knowing that it is not our own strength and will power that will accomplish this task but it is God's Holy Spirit working through us. Jesus even describes our position as His representatives on this planet as a yoke that is easy and a burden that is light in Matthew 11:30.

GOD IS ALWAYS LOVE!

The reason God's work is easy work and not a heavy task is because it is not our strength that is accomplishing the task. It is God's all-powerful strength working through us! Imagine, you have the very same Spirit that created the entire universe and all the earth living inside you. This Spirit is what gives you the strength you need to reach others everyday with God's love.

God's love is the most powerful force in the universe. Receive His unconditional love today and pour it out on others as you go about your day.

Daily Reading:
Zephaniah 3:9-20
Romans 12:9-21

Thought for the Day:
Are there people in your life that are difficult to love? Are you willing to let go and ask God to show you how you can express God's love to them and to others society deems unlovable?

Day 14 - *Accept*

"Therefore, accept each other just as Christ has accepted
you so that God will be given glory."
Romans 15:7 (NLT)

O ne of the classic scenarios of childhood rejection is
being the last kid chosen in kickball at recess. All the team
captains have picked their favorites for their teams and the
last one standing is the child left feeling rejected but
guaranteed a spot on the team with the last pick.
Fortunately, I had two older sisters who were tough so I
was well-equipped for being a top pick for kickball at an
early age. However, we all at one point or another have
been rejected in life. Maybe we didn't make the cut for the
athletic team we wanted, or we had a good date and our
counterpart didn't, or we didn't land our dream job after
an interview.

You are always God's first choice.

As a child of God, He always chooses you first to
demonstrate His kingdom here on earth. Romans 14:17
(NASB) describes God's kingdom as "not eating and
drinking, but righteousness and peace and joy in the Holy
Spirit." When we face different situations in the world God
chooses you to be the salt and light. As you walk with God
you may not realize the impact you are having on the lives
of others around you, but others can *feel* the impact you are
having on them because of the grace God has placed on
you.

GOD IS ALWAYS LOVE!

Your presence makes others feel accepted by God.

Wherever you go, because you are God's child, you carry His joy, peace, and righteousness with you. For those who don't walk with God this presence is easily noticed! Those without joy or peace can taste God's joy or peace simply because they are around you! God is always accepting of you just as you are so that you might be accepting of others just as they are.

When you are accepting towards people you encounter each day you are allowing others to experience the love of God through you. James 5:9 tells of the person who blesses God then turns and speaks ill-will toward another person who is made in the image of God. God calls us to love other people because all people are made in God's image. We all have His nose, His eyes, His ears, His arms, and resemble Him in every manner

As you show acts of kindness and love towards others what your actions are really saying to God is, "I love You, God." You tip the waitress double during rush hour at the restaurant. I love You, God. You let the person with only three groceries go in front of you at the long checkout line. I love You, Father. You stop to let the next car have the last front parking space. I love You, Jesus.

You are known by how you treat others.

Did you know that when you leave the house or leave work or school that people talk about you? They talk about what they like about you and what they don't like about you. People are always watching each other. What are people saying about you? Are you patient? Do you go out of your way to help others?

GOD IS ALWAYS LOVE!

Jesus tells us in Matthew 5:16 (NASB), "Let your light shine before men in such a way that they may see your good works, and glorify your Father who is in heaven." When you go out of your way to love and accept others, others will talk when you are not around, which is a good thing! "Yesterday she helped me get my work done early so I could make my son's game on time. *Thank God for her!*" "This weekend he volunteered at the church to help with the food pantry and no one else showed up. *Thank God for him!*"

When others know you are a Christian, and they see your good deeds they inevitably will begin to praise God for you. People who don't believe in God or may have other beliefs will be drawn to you and drawn to the God you serve. Love and accept others, day in and day out. Pray for those around you continually, and watch God begin to do a great work!

Daily Reading:
Psalm 138:1-8
Romans 15:1-12

Thought for the Day:
What are some good deeds that you have seen in others that you need to give God glory for? What are some acts of kindness, big or small, that you can practice in your daily life to show others you love and accept them?

Day 15 - *Cover*

"Above all, love each other deeply, because love covers
over a multitude of sins."
1 Peter 4:8 (NIV)

One of the greatest figures in all the Scriptures is
King David. The Bible describes David as "a man after
God's own heart" (1 Samuel 13:14). Through David's
bloodline came Jesus, the Son of God. Through David's
throne God established His eternal covenant with
mankind to redeem us from sin to live with Him forever.
Through David God conquered all Israel's enemies.
Through David the idea of building a Temple for God in
Jerusalem came.

While David accomplished incredible feats and did many
great things for God's kingdom in the Old Testament,
David commits serious sin against the Lord. In David's
weakest moment he commits adultery with Bathsheba
when he is supposed to be out at war with his enemies (2
Samuel 11). His sin grows worse when, after failed
attempts at bringing Uriah, Bathsheba's husband, and
Bathsheba together to hide an illegitimate pregnancy, he
arranges to have Uriah killed in war by placing him in the
front line of a fierce battle. David, a man after God's own
heart, has become guilty of adultery and murder of a
righteous man.

In spite of all David's shortcomings, God still receives and
loves David. David feels God's love so powerfully after his

sin that he declares in Psalm 103:12 (NCV), "He has taken our sins away from us as far as the east is from west." God loves David, forgiving him to the point of even forgetting! The prophet Micah describes God's love declaring in Micah 7:19 (NLT), "Once again You will have compassion on us. You will trample our sins under Your feet and throw them into the depths of the ocean!"

God doesn't remember your sins and neither should you.

When you ask God for forgiveness He never throws your sin back at you. He always forgives and remembers your sins and shortcomings no more. Why? Because God is love. He is nothing short of absolute, perfected love at all times! His love can cover any sin, in any magnitude, at any time because love covers everything. God promises us in 1 Corinthians 13:8 that love will never fail.

Love is always the right answer.

When we receive God's unconditional love we know how to unconditionally love others. Hebrews 8:12 (ESV) says, "For I will be merciful toward their iniquities, and I will remember their sins no more." What are your relationships like with people you see every day? Are you continually bringing up their past faults? Are they continually bringing up your past faults? Scripture tells us to love each other deeply, as we are deeply loved by God.

Giving up our right to remember each other's past faults is an act of love. When we choose to forgive and forget we are loving the way God loves. 1 Peter 4:8 says "above all" to love deeply this way. How do you overcome during that difficult season with a wayward child? Love. How do you get through to your spouse who seems distant or upset? Love. How do you get along with that difficult colleague? Love.

When you express love deeply from the heart you are overcoming the world the way Jesus overcame. The enemy of love in this world is hate. How do you respond to hate? With more love. Hate can only last for a moment, but God's love lasts forever. Never stop loving deeply!

Daily reading:
Psalm 103:1-13
1 Peter 4:8-19

Thought for the day:
When somebody wrongs you how should you respond as someone who has experienced God's love? What forgiven sins of the past do you continually replay in your mind that you need to ask God to erase?

Day 16 - *Sacrifice*

"Walk in love, as Christ loved us and gave himself up for us, a fragrant offering and sacrifice to God."
Ephesians 5:2 (ESV)

In 1997 the blockbuster film "Titanic" came out. People flocked to the theaters to see an epic love story between a poor artist named Jack and a seventeen-year-old aristocrat named Rose who met while aboard the world's largest ship, the Titanic. Most of us have heard the story about the Titanic, a magnificent British ship that tragically sank in 1912 while crossing the North Atlantic Ocean.

In the movie Jack falls in love with the soon-to-be wed Rose once aboard the ship. However, as the story goes, the marvelous ship hits a massive iceberg sinking the ship to the bottom of the ocean. Hundreds of passengers drown instantly. The remnant of survivors either make it out alive on lifeboats or are left to float on the ships remaining floating wreckage until a lifeboat comes back to rescue any remaining survivors in the freezing water.

Towards the end of the film Jack and Rose survive the sinking ship but are left swimming until a rescue lifeboat returns. A refuge of wood is all Jack and Rose have to hold on to until rescuers can come. Jack, who is madly in love with Rose, hoists Rose on top of the remaining flimsy board but selflessly stays in the freezing water to at least save Rose's life. In the last tear-jerking moments, Rose is saved but Jack freezes to death and sinks to the bottom of the sea.

The sacrifice Jack makes to save his one true love is the theme that makes Titanic one of the greatest Hollywood films of all time. Jack's sacrifice is what makes this story truly amazing! Sacrifice is defined as giving up something of great value for the sake of something that is of even greater value. Jack considered his life unworthy compared to the life of Rose. In the same way, Jesus gave up His life on the Cross as a sacrifice, making Himself sin's curse, in order to inherit you and me to be with Him forever in eternity as God's children!

Jesus died in order to inherit you as God's child forever.

The apostle Paul encourages us in Romans 12:1 to offer our bodies as a living sacrifice to God. As a *living* sacrifice it means we are continually presenting ourselves to God for His service. When you give yourself completely to God what you ultimately discover is who you really are in God's eyes and not your own.

In your own eyes you may feel insecure, unloved, inadequate, or unworthy, but in God's eyes you are strong, greatly loved, highly favored, and His biggest blessing. Once you see yourself the way God sees you then you are empowered to live life the way God intended you to.

You are called to always live blessed every day.

When you realize you are blessed 100% of the time by God, you can have confidence that any sacrifice you make for God will always be blessed and multiplied. Jesus explains how God wants to use us and multiply us with an illustration as us being branches attached to God the vine tree. He tells us in John 15:2 (NIV) that "every branch that does bear fruit He prunes so that it will be even more fruitful."

GOD IS ALWAYS LOVE!

Every sacrifice you make for God is going to be rewarded and multiplied because sacrifice is what expands His Kingdom here on earth. Like a small fruit seed in the ground that, when it dies, begins to grow into a large fruit tree that bears much fruit with many seeds, so we, when we die to our own will and plans, begin to live and grow into who God has called us to be.

Living a life of sacrifice to God is the key to living a fruitful life. Just as Christ sacrificed Himself for us so that we might live life abundantly, so we should sacrifice ourselves to help others to enable them to live life better.

Daily Reading:
Genesis 4:1-12
Ephesians 5:1-10

Thought for the Day:
What sacrifices have others made in your lifetime so that you could live life more abundantly? What sacrifices can you make so that others in your life can live life better?

Day 17 - *Give*

"Heal the sick, raise the dead, cleanse the lepers, cast out demons. Freely you received, freely give."
Matthew 10:8 (NASB)

In John 14:12 (NLT) Jesus tells His disciples, ""I tell you the truth, anyone who believes in Me will do the same works I have done, and even greater works, because I am going to be with the Father." You have the power inside you to accomplish all the works Jesus did and more. You may not always tap into this power, but as a believer in Him, you have the power within you to see miracles in this life. When Jesus died then rose from the grave He was seated at the right hand of God the Father. A few weeks after His resurrection Jesus released from Heaven what was promised, the all-powerful, miracle-working Holy Spirit.

The all-powerful Holy Spirit inside you is always at work.

When you accept Christ into your heart, God deposits His Spirit as a guarantee that you belong to Him. Before Jesus left the world He promised us concerning this guarantee in John 14:16 (ESV), "And I will ask the Father, and He will give you another Helper, to be with you forever." Jesus attributes the Holy Spirit as an eternal helper that is with us always. The promise of the Holy Spirit is the seed of promise the patriarchs of the Old Testament longed for. Why? Because God's Spirit is what gives us eternal life. Solomon describes this longing in all of mankind in

Ecclesiastes 3:11 (NIV) saying, "He has also set eternity in the human heart."

God designed you to live forever with Him.

Every time we read the gospels in the Bible Jesus refers to "seed" in His stories. What is this "seed" Jesus is talking about? The seed is the Holy Spirit, or God's word. The Holy Spirit is the seed God places inside of us so we know that we belong to Him! Paul says it this way in Romans 8:16 (NASB), "The Spirit Himself testifies with our spirit that we are children of God." The more you tap into God's Spirit that lives inside you, the more you learn how He works. God is always at work inside your heart. As you pass each test God allows you to go through He raises you to a new level in Him.

The power of the Holy Spirit is always working through you into the lives of others.

Sometimes we see God work through us in dramatic ways. That terminally ill relative you are praying for is healed overnight. The job of your dreams you thought you lost calls back and offers you the same job at an even higher salary with better benefits. That wayward child comes back to God and serves the Lord with his whole heart. Other times, God chooses to work through us slowly and steadily. These are the times God is building our character for a lifetime of godliness. When we see nothing happening we stay faithful day in and day out believing God is doing a work in our lives.

God's Spirit inside you always operates out of love.

When you walk by God's Spirit the things of God are never forced by your own strength. God always operates out of love and by you yielding to what He wants to do in each situation you face. Instead of telling God what we want Him to do, we should always ask Him what He wants to do and how we should pray accordingly. God always knows best in every situation we encounter!

Always share what God is doing in your life with others. When you do this you are stirring up the Holy Spirit in yourself and in those you are sharing with. This is when you will see God do the greater things Jesus spoke of in John 14:12!

Daily Reading:
Genesis 22:7-18
Matthew 10:1-10

Thought for the Day:
When have you experienced the Holy Spirit in a dramatic way? What is a story of a great work God has done in your life that you can share to stir up the Holy Spirit in others?

Day 18 - *Imagine*

"... No eye has seen, no ear has heard, and no mind has imagined what God has prepared for those who love Him."
1 Corinthians 2:9 (NLT)

T he human brain is the most powerful organ in our bodies. The brain gives us the power to speak, solve problems, and imagine. It controls our body temperature, blood pressure, heart rate, breathing, accepts and processes various senses of the world around us, handles our physical movements and allows us to think, reason, dream, and experience emotions. While our brain is capable of so many functions scientists estimate that we use only 10% of our mind and the other 90% remains unused. If we could tap into the other 90% of our minds what would we be capable of?

The apostle Paul addresses the power of our minds when he declares in 1 Corinthians 2:16 that we have the mind of Christ. Jesus' mind was always set on what His Father in Heaven was doing. Likewise, when we begin setting our minds on the Father's business He begins to train our minds how to think while in this world.

You always have the mind of Christ.

When you tap into the things of God your mind becomes much more powerful. God releases His knowledge and His wisdom, and you no longer make decisions only based on conventional wisdom and what the world may teach. Instead you think the way He thinks. The world says to only look out for yourself. The Lord says to also look out for your neighbor. The world says to hold on to everything you have and acquire as much as you can. The Lord says to give everything away, and He will multiply you until you overflow.

God shows us what His thinking is like when He says in James 3:17 (ESV), "But the wisdom from above is first pure, then peaceable, gentle, open to reason, full of mercy and good fruits, impartial and sincere." The Lord desires for all His children to reason and think the way He thinks. The best way to learn how God thinks is by reading His word every day. The more you know the Bible, the more you know God's character and what He really thinks about different situations.

The Bible always says exactly what God is thinking.

God has given us His word so that we will know what He thinks about anything we may be going through. As we read His word and begin to rightly apply what He shows us then we are thinking and acting just as He would think and act.

God always has a great dream to fulfill in your future.

When you train your mind to think like God thinks then He will start showing you dreams and ideas He has planned for you in your future. Once your eyes are set on Him He begins to show you things you never imagined in your wildest dreams!

Are you out of energy and feel like you've lost your fire? Press into God through reading His word and prayer.

GOD IS ALWAYS LOVE!

When you do He is releasing visions and dreams over you for you to fulfill! You will begin to see heavenly things that are from Him. 1 Corinthians 13:12 (NIV) says, "For now we see only a reflection as in a mirror; then we shall see face to face. Now I know in part; then I shall know fully, even as I am fully known."

Set your mind on the things of God, and things you never imagined possible will come to pass!

Daily Reading:
Isaiah 64:1-9
1 Corinthians 2:6-16

Thought for the Day:
What are things in your life today you never imagined possible in years past? What are some dreams hard to imagine God has placed in your heart that you know He wants to fulfill in your future?

Part Four

God Is Always Faithful!

Day 19 - *Lean*

**"Trust in the Lord with all your heart,
And lean not on your own understanding."
Proverbs 3:5 (NKJV)**

Inside each of us there is a subconscious instinct that guides us about our day for our well-being. When you walk across the road and turn both ways checking for oncoming traffic without thought, you are using your instinct. When you are about to make a purchase in the store but something tells you not yet, then you find the exact same thing on sale half off one store over, you are listening to your instinct. Usually our instincts guide us correctly but sometimes we misjudge.

God will always guide you correctly.

As you read God's word every day, storing up His promises for your life, you are depositing His truth which confirms your conscience that you are being guided the right direction in life. The more of God's word you have in your life, the more you can lean on His understanding to make decisions. The culture may tell you something is right when it is really a violation of God's word, and other times culture may tell you something is wrong when really God approves and encourages it.

Cultural norms come and go, but God's word lasts forever.

GOD IS ALWAYS FAITHFUL!

Isaiah 40:8 (NLV) says, "The grass dries up. The flower loses its color. But the Word of our God stands forever." Sometimes we go through life and we come across things that causes us frustration or confusion. We see something on TV that contradicts our value system or hear something on the radio that doesn't make sense. Things we used to believe were right we aren't so sure of anymore and the things we thought were taboo are up for compromise. Sometimes the voice of the culture and what you are hearing every day is in direct opposition to what God says in the Bible. You no longer know how you feel about situations you once firmly believed in.

Your emotions change, but God's truth never changes.

As imperfect people how we feel about certain issues on any given day are subject to change. Some days you may wake up on the wrong side of the bed and everything is wrong with the world! Other days you may wake up excited looking forward to a productive, fun day. However, as we grow in our walks with God certain truths should be set in our hearts that never change.

As God's child you were born with a conscience. When you align your thoughts and values with God's thoughts and values found in His word then God promises you will be filled with love that is pure and unquestionable. Timothy instructs us in this in 1 Timothy 1:5 (NLT) saying, "The purpose of my instruction is that all believers would be filled with love that comes from a pure heart, a clear conscience, and genuine faith."

Do you have a hard time showing love to others? Read God's word and store it in your heart. The more you learn His word the more it will come out of you effortlessly. God promises that as you store up His word in your heart and mind that His word will not return empty (Isaiah 55:11). Instead your life will overflow with the fruits of love, joy, peace, patience, goodness, kindness, faithfulness, gentleness, and self-control! (Galatians 5:22-23)

Instead of leaning on your understanding and how you feel about different situations, lean on God and His word, trusting that His word is eternal and can always be trusted. Others' words and opinions will fail you, and your own understanding will fail you, but God's word and His love will never fail!

Daily Reading:
Proverbs 3:1-12
Galatians 5:16-26

Thought for the Day:
What are values you frequently see portrayed on TV and in the media that you know contradict what God says? How do you think God wants to use you to change unbiblical messages in the culture to positively impact the lives of others?

Day 20 - *Carry*

"Even when you are old, I will be the same. Even when your hair has turned gray, I will take care of you. I made you and will take care of you. I will carry you and save you."
Isaiah 46:4 (NCV)

T he best retirement package you can invest in now is God's kingdom. Material possessions and money can only temporarily provide you physical safety and meet your needs, but following God will not only fulfill your life while you are alive today but also will fill your treasury in Heaven which God has stored up just for you. When you tend to the things of God He promises He will attend to and supersede all your needs before you even ask! This doesn't mean you should stop saving up for retirement after your working years, but it does mean you should consider carefully how you invest your time and resources.

Are you tithing to the church that's expanding God's kingdom and teaching the Word? Are you reaching out to your neighbors? Are you going on mission trips or supporting others who are reaching people in some of the most difficult places in the world?

You are always God's missionary in this world.

Whether you have been on a mission trip or lived somewhere foreign as a missionary or not, God has called you to be a missionary to the world you are currently in.

GOD IS ALWAYS FAITHFUL!

Are you deeply involved in a career? Your mission field is your colleagues and those you do business with. Are you a teacher? Your mission field is the students you teach. Are you a student? Your mission field is your fellow peers. Are you a stay-at-home parent? Your mission field is implanting God's truth in your children and raising up the next generation of leaders.

Jesus' last command to His disciples is found in Matthew 28:19 (ESV), "Go therefore and make disciples of all nations..." As followers of Christ, we are all commissioned to "go". This may look different for each of us as all of our lives and experiences are vastly different, but God has a calling on each of our lives to go and share His truth and His unconditional love.

God is always faithful, even to the end.

When you invest a lifetime of following God, abiding in His love and His word, He promises to take care of you when you grow older. Being tended to by Almighty God is the best retirement package you can sign up for! When you have put Him first in your life, Isaiah 64:4 promises that God will take care of you even in your old age.

In the Scriptures the Hebrew people were know for being shepherds. Many Scriptures throughout the Bible refer to God as the Shepherd and we as His sheep. When we give our lives to Christ we are saying we are no longer going our own way, but we are now a part of God's flock and are following Him wherever He leads us as the Shepherd of our hearts.

God is always carrying you.

GOD IS ALWAYS FAITHFUL!

Psalm 68:19 (NLT) says, "Praise the Lord; praise God our Savior! For each day He carries us in His arms." The Lord is carrying us in His arms every day of our lives! As sheep we sometimes go astray, but God, being the Faithful Shepherd, always comes back for us and carries us to His flock. When life seems out of control or things don't make sense, you can always have confidence that God has you in His arms carrying you to your destination. You are never out of His reach because you are *always* in His arms.

Thank God today for being the Good and Faithful Shepherd! Praise Him always for keeping you close and carrying you to your destiny!

Daily Reading:
Isaiah 46:3-13
Matthew 28:9-20

Thought for the Day:
Who are the people in your mission field you feel God is calling you to reach out to? What areas of your life do you feel are out of your control that you need to trust God is already carrying in His arms?

Day 21- *Walk*

"Even though I walk through the valley of the shadow of death, I fear no evil, for You are with me; Your rod and Your staff, they comfort me." Psalm 23:4 (NASB)

In the Scriptures God is referred to as our shepherd. The most important pieces of equipment a shepherd carries are his rod and staff. The shepherd's rod is made of hard wood and about as long as the shepherd's arm. The rod is used to protect the sheep from danger. The shepherd's staff is longer, more slender, and hook shaped at the top and is used primarily for steering the sheep. Jesus tells us in John 10:11 (NIV), "I am the Good Shepherd. The Good Shepherd lays down His life for the sheep." As the shepherd of our hearts and lives, Jesus uses His heavenly rod and staff to protect, correct, lead, and guide us in our walks with Him.

The Lord is always directing your footsteps.

Proverbs 20:24 (NIV) says, "A person's steps are directed by the LORD. How then can anyone understand their own way?" When you begin walking in step with God everyday, you are no longer relying on your own intellect and reason to make decisions. Instead you make decisions based on what God tells you in His word and by what His Spirit inside you prompts you to do.

The Lord says to be quick to listen and slow to speak (James 1:19) so instead of always interrupting people in conversation with all you want to say you begin to listen to what others are saying. The Lord says to be good to your enemies and bless those who curse you (Luke 6:27-28) so instead of hurling an insult back at the person who just made a cutting remark toward you, you smile, ignoring the negative comment, and respond with kindness knowing love always trumps hate.

When you are walking off course the Lord will always draw you back to where you need to be.

As you go through life, sometimes you may find yourself drifting away from what you know you should be doing. This is the time to call out to God your Father and know He is there ready to guide you back to where you need to be. Maybe you have the wrong friends in your life, you're living in a compromised lifestyle, or you're neglecting your time with the Lord by missing church or not reading the Word.

Now is always the time to return to the Lord.

Right now is always a good time to seek God. By saying a genuine prayer, calling that faithful friend, opening the Bible to your favorite passage, or attending a good church again you are inviting God to shepherd your life. The Lord promises that He will always usher in life and blessings *today* when you willfully choose Him in Deuteronomy 30:19 (NLT) saying, "Today I have given you the choice between life and death, between blessings and curses. Now I call on heaven and earth to witness the choice you make. Oh, that you would choose life, so that you and your descendants might live!"

Your obedience always blesses your loved ones.

GOD IS ALWAYS FAITHFUL!

When you obey the Lord, His blessings not only overtake you, but they also overtake your spouse, your children, your parents, your siblings, your best friends, your colleagues, and anyone else that is in your life. Your life is like a cup that God pours His blessings into until His blessings overflow (Psalm 23:5) . The overflow is meant to spill out into your neighbors' cups until their lives overflow with God's goodness!

A revival of God's goodness always starts with you.

Do you long to see a revival of God's goodness in your life and the lives of others? In the life of your community, city, or region? Seek God and His promises. As you learn what pleases the Lord and do what He asks you to do His goodness is surely going to chase you down and overtake you and those around you!

Daily reading:
Psalm 23:1-6
John 10:7-18

Thought for the Day:
What are some areas of your life you know are off course in God's plan for your life? What are steps you can take to draw closer to God as He leads you?

Day 22 - *Confess*

"If we confess our sins, He is faithful and just to forgive us our sins and to cleanse us from all unrighteousness."
1 John 1:9 (ESV)

W henever we mess up God is not waiting with a big stick in Heaven ready to punish us. On the contrary, with every right step God is looking to bless and increase us. God is interested in expanding His kingdom through you. He comforts us in our weakness and corrects us when we are straying from Him, but He is never "out to get us". The devil is the accuser of sin, not the Lord (Revelation 12:10).

The Bible tells us that our sin is what separates us from God. Isaiah 59:2 (NLT) says, "It's your sins that have cut you off from God. Because of your sins, He has turned away and will not listen anymore." Fortunately, we now have an advocate through His Son Jesus Christ who walked in the flesh as fully man and fully God and can sympathize with all of our weaknesses!

When you confess your sins to God, He is always faithful to forgive you!

The first step to coming into a right relationship with God is accepting His Son Jesus into your life and confessing your sin to the Lord. One of the most liberating experiences you can have is handing God all your shortcomings so He can replace them with His incredible power! Whatever your struggle is, financial hardships, relationships, work, school, believing, or an addictive temptation, God promises He can set you free when you come to Him. Jesus declares in John 8:36 (NIV), "So if the Son sets you free, you will be free indeed."

The instant you get in agreement with God and what He says, confessing all that is in your heart to Him, He can set you free from that troubling spirit! The name of Jesus is the only name in this world that has authority over *everything*. Do you need to be healed in your body, mind, or spirit? Speak His name over that area of suffering. Do you need a breakthrough in your finances, work, or school? Speak His name over that area of resistance. Do you need restoration in a marriage, family, or relationship? Keep speaking His name over that person every day.

Confess Jesus' name and He will take all authority over every area of your life.

In Matthew 28:18 Jesus tells us *all* authority in heaven and on earth has been given to Him. When you acknowledge what He has done, dying for your sins on the Cross so that you might walk in freedom from sin, then you are willfully accepting His authority to go to work in your life *right now*. Confession is the most powerful weapon the Lord has given us against the enemy. God says demons tremble in terror when they hear the name of Jesus (James 2:19).

Confess Jesus' name and the enemy always has to leave now!

Remember, when you accepted Christ into your life, the enemy could no longer legally possess anything in your life that belongs to you. When you see the enemy try to rise up against you in any area, whether it be work, family, school, friends, material belongings, or anything else involving you, you can immediately go to the throne of

GOD IS ALWAYS FAITHFUL!

God in prayer and command the enemy to leave. Everything you have belongs to the name of Jesus and everything Jesus has He has freely given back to you because you are in Him!

Every knee will bow and every tongue will confess Jesus is Lord.

Paul tells of a day when all of mankind will bow to Jesus and confess Him to God as Lord over all. Romans 14:11 (NKJV) says, "As I live, says the Lord, every knee shall bow to Me, and every tongue shall confess to God." Whether or not we choose today to confess Jesus, or after this life, is our decision. Only those who choose Him now will be with Him forever. Choose Jesus today!

Daily Reading:
Isaiah 59:11-21
1 John 1:1-10

Thought for the Day:
What are things in your heart you need to confess to God so He can forgive and heal you? What are voices of the accuser you need to take authority over and kick out of your mind?

Day 23 - *Praise*

"For He loves us with unfailing love; the LORD's faithfulness endures forever. Praise the LORD!"
Psalm 117:2 (NLT)

Whether you are having the best day of your life or the worst day of the century you should always praise the Lord. When things are going well, praise the Lord! When everything seems to be going wrong, praise the Lord! When not much is going on, praise the Lord! We were designed to worship God at all times. When we are bringing Him praise and giving Him all the glory we are fulfilling our purpose! Jesus tells us that praising Him is always appropriate. Luke 19:40 even says that if we don't worship Him the rocks will cry out in worship!

Keep praise on your lips always.

Psalm 22:3 (NCV) says, "You sit as the Holy One. The praises of Israel are Your throne." Where does the Lord sit? On your praises! When you worship God you are inviting Him to physically come into your presence. Praising Him is one way we stir up our faith for God to do something amazing in our lives. If you are looking for your miracle praise God and let Him transform you by being in His presence.

The more you praise God the more you experience His presence.

Listening to praise music is incredibly powerful in your walk with God. The more you listen to Him being praised, the more His praises will be on your mind and heart throughout the day. Psalm 19:14 (NLT) says, "May the words of my mouth and the meditation of my heart be pleasing to You, O LORD, my Rock and my Redeemer." When you meditate on God's word and hear His praises throughout the day you are filling your spirit with the knowledge of God.

Praise enables you to know and experience God more fully.

Many times we read God's word and intellectually comprehend what God is saying, but when we sing God's word it stirs our spirit in a much deeper way. Worship is where God lives. In Revelation 4:5-11 the apostle John gives us a glimpse of God's throne in Heaven where God is worshipped day and night without ceasing. Singing God's praises is how you experience Heaven on earth!

Scientists have discovered that singing lowers stress, raises endorphin levels, and relieves anxious thoughts. When you are overwhelmed by challenges in the day, take a moment and sing to the Lord. It doesn't have to be loud. Hum under your breathe while you are at your desk or take a short drive to sing and worship God in your car. When you do this, you are praising God in whatever storm you are in.

Praising the Lord tramples the enemy's power of darkness at work against you. Ephesians 6:12 (NCV) tells us, "Our fight is not against people on earth but against the rulers and authorities and the powers of this world's darkness, against the spiritual powers of evil in the heavenly world." Every battle you face is spiritual. What you physically see is not permanent, but what is happening in the spiritual realm is eternal. Singing God's praises drives out darkness and fills your life with God's light!

GOD IS ALWAYS FAITHFUL!

Praise the Lord because He is always faithful!

God has promised He will never leave us nor forsake us (Deuteronomy 31:6). He has promised we will live with Him for eternity, and no one can take us from Him (John 10:28). He has promised He will never stop loving us (Psalm 117:2). He has promised we are always blessed as we praise Him (Psalm 84:4). Never stop praising Him for Who He is and all His wonderful promises!

Daily Reading:
Psalm 117:1-118:9
Luke 19:28-40

Thought for the Day:
What is your favorite worship song? When is the best time of day you can set aside to personally worship God by singing His praises?

Day 24 - *Grow*

**"Then the way you live will always honor and please the
Lord, and your lives will produce every kind of good
fruit. All the while, you will grow as you learn to know
God better and better."**
Colossians 1:10 (NLT)

T he last teaching I ever heard in college was from a
professor who talked about the meaning of life. I had spent
six years studying in undergraduate and graduate school,
and it all boiled down to this one question: What is the
purpose of life? Years of hard earned knowledge from
reading textbooks, listening to lectures, and taking exams,
and this was the last thing our professor wanted us to
remember before we graduated and entered the "real
world". He picked up a piece of chalk and wrote four big
letters on the board: G-R-O-W

For the next hour he talked about life's meaning is for us to
grow. No matter where you are in life, God designed you
to always grow. "When you stop learning, you stop
growing," the professor concluded. In other words, never
stop learning. If you want to grow in any area of life, you
must continue to fill yourself with knowledge in that area.

*As you learn more about God through reading His word, you
will grow accordingly.*

Reading the Bible is imperative to your walk with God!
Colossians 1:10 tells us the more we read the Bible the

more we will grow. If you feel stagnant in your walk with God, or even unworthy, read His word and discover what *He says* about you. The promises all throughout Scripture concerning you are unfathomable and much greater than anything the world can offer! His word can help you make better decisions, cure incurable diseases, resolve unresolvable issues, and give you favor in ways you never dreamed of.

No other book ever written in human history can promise you eternal life, an abundant life *now*, and supernatural power to overcome any obstacle through God. As God asks Sarah in Genesis 18:14 (NIV), "Is anything too hard for the LORD?". The obvious answer is, of course not! He is God, Creator of the universe, heaven, earth, and everything within them! Learn who God is by studying His word continually, and you will never stop growing.

Never stop reading the Bible, and you will never stop growing.

Jesus always taught directly from His knowledge of the Scriptures. Over and over Jesus refers to the Old Testament prophets, Torah (Law of Moses), and kings of Israel in His teachings and sermons. He knew the word of God and ushered in the new and better covenant prophesied of in the Old Testament (Jeremiah 31:31-34). By accepting Jesus Christ, you have entered into an eternal, unbreakable covenant with God. The New Testament testifies about this new covenant through the writings of the apostles, and those who walked with Jesus.

When you accept Jesus and His word, you are set free from the Law of the Old Testament, which condemns sinners and lawbreakers to death (which is all of us because no one is perfect, except Jesus Christ). The Law given to Moses in the Old Testament is good, but it cannot make us righteous in God's eyes (Galatians 2:21). Only Jesus, the Lamb of God, can permanently take away all our sins so we can stand before God for eternity.

Accept the seed of God's word, share it with others, and He will always be faithful to cause the growing.

God promises He will always be faithful to grow us through the seed of His word; He also promises to reward us when we share the Bible and the truth of all He has done for us with others (1 Corinthians 3:6-9). Sometimes sharing the seed of God's word can be as simple as telling your lunch buddy how God is working in your life or by sharing your favorite Bible verses with your friends and family members. Your story about what God has done can be powerful enough to change the life of that friend or acquaintance you are sharing with. Sharing is how you plant the seed of God in the lives of others.

You are never too young or too old to begin reading and learning the word of God. We are all lifelong learners of God's word, and our spirits always have room to grow until the day we meet Him in eternity. Make up your mind to be a lifelong learner and never stop growing!

Daily Reading:
Genesis 18:9-19
Colossians 1:9-20

Thought for the Day:
Do you consider yourself a lifelong learner? If not, how can you make changes to become one? What is a "seed" in God's word or a personal story you think God wants you to share with others in order to grow His kingdom?

Part Five

God Is Always Your Father!

Day 25 - *Return*

**"Let us examine our ways and test them,
and let us return to the Lord."
Lamentations 3:40 (NIV)**

One of the most heartfelt stories in all of Scriptures is the story of the Prodigal Son in Luke 15. Jesus tells the parable of how a young son squanders the wealth of his inheritance from his father with wild living in a foreign place. Inevitably, the wayward son becomes completely broke and hungry, so he hires himself out to foreigners to feed pigs during a severe famine. Luke 15:17 says "when he came to his senses" he realizes he could at least approach his father back home for work as a hired hand, as he believes he was no longer worthy to be called his father's son.

As the son journeys home, his father sees him a long way off and is immediately filled with compassion. The father sprints to meet his son, embracing and kissing him! The son begins to tell his father how he has greatly sinned and that he is no longer worthy to be called his son, but the father immediately begins giving orders to the servants to bring *his son* the best robe in the house, a ring of authority for his hand, and sandals that only noble feet can wear! Furthermore, the father orders to have the finest cattle cooked for dinner for a celebration of his son's return home.

107

GOD IS ALWAYS YOUR FATHER!

When Jesus tells this story He drives home several points. How many of us can relate to this wayward child who has come home? The answer, of course, is all of us. We have all at one point or another in our lives strayed away from God our Father. Jesus also tells this story so we will understand the heart of the Father when we return to Him, even after all our shortcomings and failures. One of God's greatest attributes is His heart of compassion. Our God is a very compassionate God who longs for all of us to return to Him so He can love us and fill our lives with His very best!

When you return to God, He always treats you as Heaven's highest priority as His child.

When you make a decision in your life to return to God with all your heart, you are ushering in God's love and His heavenly kingdom to go to work on your behalf. Heaven is celebrating your return! Luke 15:7 tells us that there is great joy in Heaven when anyone returns to Him! How do you return to Him? Repent.

The word repent is defined as a change of mind towards God. "Re-" meaning "to return", and "pent" meaning "the highest place". You are changing your thoughts from earthly, sinful thoughts upward to heavenly, godly thoughts, looking to please the Lord. When you repent, you are changing your way of thinking. Repenting also requires you have a change of heart, where you regret walking in sinful ways against God and take steps toward walking in the things of God. When you repent, God always forgives you. He already saw you coming a long way off and is ready to run and embrace you with His immeasurable love!

You are always called your Father's child.

108

GOD IS ALWAYS YOUR FATHER!

When you return to your Father, you are His child forever. You may have got off track in life, seeking your own pleasures and forsaking the good things God had in store for you, but now you are ready to return home. The best decision you can make for yourself, for your children, for your spouse, and for your loved ones is to return to God. When you do, God will wash your dark stained sins white as snow! His blessings will pour out on you and overflow into the lives of all those around you!

Return to your Father with all your heart. Give Him every area of your life. Trust Him and know that He is always good. He is always fighting your battles for you. You are always called His daughter or son. He is always your Father!

Daily Reading:
Lamentations 3:31-41
Luke 15:11-24

Thought for the Day:
Have you ever experienced a time of repenting before the Lord for something you have done in the past? Are there things you need to repent of today so God can give you His best in return?

Day 26 - *Seek*

W hen I was a child, each year on Easter Sunday
my family and I would attend church then have a huge
family Easter egg hunt afterward. The grownups would
spend hours before church hiding plastic Easter eggs full
of all sorts of candy, toys, and small amounts of money in
the backyard. All the kids could hardly sit still during the
service, as we had our minds fixed on all the goodies we
would acquire in the ensuing annual hunt (and from the
excitement of Jesus being raised from the dead, of
course!!).

While all the children enjoyed accumulating as much
candy and eggs as they could fit in their Easter egg
baskets, everybody always wanted to find the golden egg.
The golden egg was different than all the other eggs. It was
the only gold-colored egg, larger than all the rest, and most
importantly, it always had a $100 bill in it! To find the
golden egg was to discover the ultimate prize on this
adventurous hunt!

However, unlike all the other eggs, it was always the most
well-hidden. So well-hidden, it might take until dusk for
somebody to find the egg! And if nobody had found the

egg by sunset, clues were given (as somebody had to find the egg before Easter supper). Whoever found the egg had bragging rights for years to come, as the golden egg was almost impossible to find.

While we may consider things like Easter egg hunts childish fun, the Bible actually teaches just the opposite. In fact, God compares hunting out hidden treasures as a duty only fit for kings. Proverbs 25:2 (ESV) says, "It is the glory of God to conceal things, but the glory of kings is to search things out."

God always rewards those who seek Him.

God is a God who offers incentives and rewards for those seeking His will. He never commissions you to do something without a reward in exchange. We obey Him because we love Him, but God *expects* us to seek reward from Him, just as a child seeks a reward from a parent or teacher. Hebrews 11:6 (NIV) says, "And without faith it is impossible to please God, because anyone who comes to Him must believe that He exists and that He rewards those who earnestly seek Him."

When you seek God He promises both tangible and intangible blessings. He has promised His spirit of love, peace, joy, and other blessings will flow like a river from within your spirit. He also promises material blessings. In the New Testament, much conflict arose within the church because of a lack of resources. The apostle James admonishes the church for not seeking God first, saying, "You have not because you ask not!" The Lord wants you to seek Him for *all* your needs!

Do you lack peace in your heart about your eternal destination? Ask God to show you the immovable helmet of salvation He has already placed on your head (Ephesians 6:17). Jesus has promised it is impossible for anyone to pluck you out of your Father's hand (John 10:29)! Do you feel like life is a battle for surviving, when deep within you know you were made to thrive? Take hold of John 10:10 and know Jesus promises abundance of life is on its way! Declare Deuteronomy 28:1-2. God is setting you high above the nations, and His blessings are chasing you down to overtake you!

You were made to soar in the promises of God! He designed you to seek Him and expect those explosive blessings to come into your life. Loved ones turn their hearts back to God, that new home mortgage finally goes through, that dream job finally comes to pass, the keys to that new car that doesn't break down every week is finally yours, that person of your dreams who treats you right walks into your life, that opportunity to go back and finish college is now available. God wants you to flourish as you seek Him!

Seek God first in all you do, and He promises He will reward you with His favor, with His promotions, and with things much greater than you could ever ask, think, or imagine!

Daily Reading:
Deuteronomy 4:29-40
Hebrews 11:1-11

Thought for the Day:
When is a time you sought the Lord's will first and later on saw that His answer was much better than anything you could have thought of? What is an area you are experiencing lack in that you need to ask God for more of?

Day 27 - *Receive*

**"But to all who did receive Him, who believed in His
name, He gave the right to become children of God."
John 1:12 (ESV)**

God's love is the central message of the Bible. All
sixty-six books from Genesis to Revelation tell one
continuous story of God's love and redemption of
mankind. *God loves you.* Get that deep into your spirit. God
created you in order to love you and to have fellowship
with you. The most important part of your walk with God
is learning to *receive* God's love. When you receive God's
love and experience how much He loves you it enables
you to love others the way God your Father loves.

*You must receive the Father's love before you know how to love
others.*

Receiving and walking in God's love fulfills every
command given in the Scriptures (Galatians 5:14). Some of
us may have difficulty receiving God the Father's love due
to an unhealthy upbringing by an absent or abusive
parent. Others may struggle with believing God loves
them because of a painful past. Whatever obstacles are
blocking your heart from receiving God's love, let them go.
Let go of the bitterness, disappoints, and any
unforgiveness in your heart. God isn't asking you to deny
the pain, but He is asking you to trust Him to heal you.
Isaiah 61:1 says He sent Christ to bind up and heal any
brokenness in your heart.

GOD IS ALWAYS YOUR FATHER!

Hebrews 12:1 (NASB) says, "Let us also lay aside every encumbrance and the sin which so easily entangles us, and let us run with endurance the race that is set before us." In other words, let go of the sins of the past so you can be free to move forward in life. So many people never realize their full potential because they become in bondage to regret, bitterness, and self-hatred. If you will let go of the chains of the past you can move forward into the great plans God has in your future.

The more you receive God's love, the more you are set free to love yourself and others.

In order to love your neighbor *as yourself*, you must first love yourself. You cannot love others the way God intends you to if you don't first learn to love yourself. Is there anything about you that you despise or beat yourself up over? God made you in His image. You are fearfully and wonderfully made! Whatever God has already spoken over you, you should speak over yourself.

The enemy does not want you to believe God loves you or loves to bless you. On the contrary, the enemy has come to kill, steal, and destroy your identity as a child of God. Don't agree with the negative thoughts from the enemy; rather, get in agreement with what God says about you. God says you are an overcomer. God says you are free. God says you are the head and not the tail. God says you are a child of the Most High God and heir of all things in Jesus Christ.

God says because you received His Son Jesus, you are His child forever.

This means you have every right to all things in God's kingdom. You have a right to heal and be healed. You have a right to love and receive love. You have a right to live and not die. Because you are the bride of Christ, you are grafted into God's family. He is your Father who is the Creator of all things, and you get it all!

Daily Reading:
Isaiah 61:1-11
John 1:9-18

Thought for the Day:
What are things in your heart you need to let go of so you can receive more of God's love? What are some of the rights you have as God's child that you need to take hold of?

Day 28 - *Call*

**"I call upon the LORD, Who is worthy to be praised,
And I am saved from my enemies."
Psalm 18:3 (NASB)**

One of the most powerful forces in all of nature during summertime is a thunderstorm. I have always been amazed at how quickly the climate can dramatically change from a hot summer day to a cool, windy storm full of thunder, lightning, and rain! As the warm, moist air of the ground begins to rapidly rise upward the air cools, condenses and quickly forms massive storm clouds (known as cumulonimbus clouds). These cumulonimbus clouds can rise 12 miles or higher!

Strong updrafts and downdrafts within the cloud cause incredibly powerful electrical charges from within the cloud, and between the cloud and the earth's surface, creating lightning. Lightning flashes cause air molecules to expand rapidly producing sound waves we hear as thunder. Meteorologists estimate an average thunderstorm expends enough energy equal to 50 atomic bombs!

In Psalm 18, King David compares calling on God in a time of need to stirring up a powerful thunderstorm against your enemies in the unseen spiritual realm. David describes God as standing on dark storm clouds, soaring on the winds, speaking with a voice of thunder, and hurling lightning like arrows at his enemies, sending them into confusion. When you call on God for help, you are inviting a thunderstorm of His power over your enemies.

The more you pray, the more you are generating a storm in the heavenly realms for God to move on your behalf.

When dark forces come against you in your walk with God, you can always call on your Father for help.

The more you pray into that heated problem, that heavenly cumulonimbus cloud begins to start forming. You pray a little more, that thunder cloud rises even higher. You keep praying, and before long that cloud is 8, 10, 12 miles higher in the skies, then all of the sudden you see a drop of rain on that situations. The sky grows darker, the winds pick up speed, and that situation begins to shift. Keep calling on the Lord. Pick up the phone. Keep dialing His number. Remind Him of His word. Declare who God is. Watch the Lord drop 50 atomic bombs of His power on your enemies in the spiritual realm! Expect those mountains to fall before the Lord!

A thunderstorm of God's power is coming! He is moving mountains on your behalf. The power of that addiction begins to break. What used to be difficult is now anointed with ease. That wayward child begins to show signs of returning back to God. That anxiety and depression begin to be swept away by the winds of God's peace. Release your faith, and watch the Lord drop 50 atomic bombs of His power on that mountain of injustice.

Through Jesus you always have authority over the enemy, who is the devil.

The more you walk with God, the more the enemy will attempt to oppose you. 1 Peter 4:12 (NLT) says, "Dear friends, don't be surprised at the fiery trials you are going through, as if something strange were happening to you." The enemy does not want you to prosper in the things of

God. If he cannot stop you from going to church, he will try to keep you from praying and reading God's word. If he cannot keep you from praying and reading, he will try to send destruction into your life.

Hebrews 2:14 tells us that Jesus conquered Satan and death when He died and came to life again. The enemy came to place mountains of trouble in your life, but God tells us we have authority to speak to those mountains. Psalm 97:5 (NIV) even says, "The mountains melt like wax before the LORD, before the Lord of all the earth." When we set that mountain of problems before God, He promises those problems will melt away in His presence. He flattens those problems and before long all we see left is His light shining through in the way which we should go.

Focus on God and His presence, and the actions we need to take become much more obvious because we are no longer focused on the problems but on the Lord and His power. Call on the Lord in times of difficulty. Speak His name, and the enemy must flee!

Daily Reading:
Psalm 18:6-19
1 Peter 4:12-19

Thought for the Day:
What are situations in your life that you need to begin praying over for God's power to come and change things? Are there people in your life in need of a cumulonimbus cloud of God's power to shift things in their favor, and you need to pray for today?

Day 29 - *Choose*

"Choose for yourselves this day whom you will serve...
As for me and my house, we will serve the Lord."
Joshua 24:15 (NKJV)

Every day you make thousands of choices. You choose what to eat, who you are going to hang out with, where you are going to sit, whether or not you are going to make that phone call. The choices you make each day affect your future. As you make decisions, you are taking steps either towards something that gives life or takes away life. After giving God's law to Israel, Moses tells the Israelites in Deuteronomy 30:19 (NIV), "I have set before you life and death, blessings and curses. Now choose life, so that you and your children may live." In this world you can choose to bless or to curse any situation you come across. When you choose to bless you give life.

God always gives you two choices in this world. Choose life.

When you make decisions, choose things that will help build you and others up as you go about your day. Put on a positive attitude and outlook on life. When you see someone struggling through the day at work or school, intentionally go out of your way to give that person a kind and encouraging word. When you are having a difficult day, instead of cursing everyone and everything for all your problems, speak the blessing. Choose life-giving words to change your situation.

When you choose life day by day, week by week, your world will begin to look different. Your life will be full of life-giving blessings and many of the obstacles you faced in the past will begin to fade away. You will have more energy to get things done than you did in the past. You will have more confidence to accomplish the big dreams God has placed inside you. You will rub off on the people around you; before long, they will begin to speak the blessings too! Choosing to be a life-giver is contagious!

When you choose life, you are really choosing to have life God's way. Jesus says in John 14:6 (NLT), "I am the Way, the Truth, and the Life. No one can come to the Father except through Me." Jesus is the only true source of all life. The Scriptures tells us that all of life was created through Him (Colossians 1:16). The more you become like your Creator, Jesus Christ, the more you are going to give life to your God-given dreams and to the dreams of others.

You are always serving God when you are serving others.

When you serve others, you are being one of God's life-givers. Jesus tells His disciples in Mark 10:43 that whoever wants to be greatest will first become a servant. Jesus teaches the principle of having a servant's heart. When you serve others, you are giving life to their goals and dreams.

Serving others is a conscious choice. Before you start your day, think of others you know you may come across. How can you serve them the way Christ has served us? What is an encouraging word that you can speak into that person's life? Maybe you can make your server's busy morning better with a smile and an extra tip, or you can bless your busy co-worker by showing up a little earlier and having everything set up for business on time.

GOD IS ALWAYS YOUR FATHER!

Servanthood is a way of life in Heaven. Mark 10:45 (NIV) tells us, "For even the Son of Man did not come to be served, but to serve, and to give his life as a ransom for many." Think of a culture where everyone serves one another in love. Think of a day when all of us put the needs of others before ourselves. This is Jesus' desire for what His church is to look like. Serving one another is a glimpse of Heaven on earth!

Daily Reading:
Joshua 24:14-25
Mark 10:35-45

Thought for the Day:
As a life-giver, what are blessings you need to start speaking over your life and the lives of others? Who all can you serve in order to help bring their dreams to pass?

Day 30 - Feed

"He said to him the third time, 'Simon, son of John, do
you love Me?' ...and he said to Him, 'Lord, You know
everything; You know that I love You.' Jesus said to him,
'Feed My sheep.'"
John 21:17 (ESV)

In the Old Testament the prophet Ezekiel spoke out
against the leaders of Israel for neither caring for their
Jewish brothers and sisters nor for the things of God.
Instead the leaders were only caring for themselves at the
expense of the people. In Ezekiel 34:8 the prophet declares
God is bringing calamity on the leaders, or shepherds, of
Israel for only feeding themselves and not caring for the
rest of God's people, also referred to as the flock of sheep.

Unfortunately, even in Biblical days, many of the leaders
abused their power, living in comfort and luxury at the
expense of their subjects. A few great leaders of the Old
Testament, like Gideon, David, Hezekiah, and Nehemiah,
did not abuse their position of authority but used it to
bring justice and bless many. Nehemiah even notes in
Nehemiah 5:15 that he refused to oppress others for
financial gain as former governors over Judah had because
of his fear of God.

As leaders representing God, to neglect God's children is a
serious offense against God, just as society today would
deem parents or authority figures who neglect their
children's well-being as a serious offense. However, there
was no CPS service number to call in the Old Testament,

but God did raise up prophets and other people who followed Him to make things right.

Helping tend to God's people is the mark of a mature Christian.

When Jesus tells Simon Peter in John 21 to feed His sheep, Jesus is also addressing leaders today. Jesus wants each of us to grow spiritually so that we can one day take care of His people as a leader. You may never pastor a church or lead the gospel choir, but you do have a calling to serve somewhere in the Body of Christ. What are your gifts? How can God use your gifts to bless others?

When you use your gifts for God to bless others, you are feeding His sheep.

One of the best ways to discover your gifts for God's people is first by joining a community of believers who are pursuing God just as you are. When you go through life you are going to need help along the way to get you where you need to go. God has ordained us to have fellowship with one another so we can serve each other with our gifts and talents.

If you are in a position of leadership or are about to step into a position of leadership, whether at a church, in the business community, at school, or in a government office, the Lord has called you to be in that position of power to make a positive influence on the lives of many. Being in a position of power should humble us!

Like Jesus, true leaders are to first serve before being served.

As a leader, your calling is to make sure the needs of those subject to you are met. Abusing your power or lording your authority is never pleasing to the Lord. God has called us to be even more humble when we are in a position of influence, and not dominating. When you put the needs of others first, especially when in a position of authority, God's favor will pour out on you even more to help you accomplish great things in the lives of many and expand His kingdom!

Daily Reading:
Ezekiel 34:7-17
John 21:15-25

Thought for the Day:
What are some of your God-given gifts that you can use to feed God's sheep? Who is a leader you can faithfully pray for that is leading God's people?

Day 31 - Create

"So God created human beings in His own image. In the image of God He created them; male and female He created them. Then God blessed them…"
Genesis 1:27-28 (NLT)

At the beginning of time, Adam and Eve, your biological ancestors and oldest grandparents, were created directly by the physical hand of God to do good works. After creating everything in six days, God relocated Adam to the Garden of Eden in order to tend to the garden and enjoy fellowship with Him. Shortly thereafter God fashioned Eve from Adam's rib while he was in a deep sleep after naming all the animals. Notice, from the beginning of time, God had a purpose for mankind and His creation. For Adam and Eve it was tending to the Garden of Eden, having fellowship with Him, raising children, and taking dominion over the earth.

Now, under the new covenant in Jesus, we are "born again" spiritually speaking in order to tend to the things of God and have fellowship with God the Father through His Son Jesus Christ. When you accepted Christ to come abide in you, you agreed to deny your own will in order to discover the best life God has for you (which is much greater than anything you could imagine for yourself!). 2 Corinthians 5:17 (NIV) tells us, "Therefore, if anyone is in Christ, the new creation has come: The old has gone, the new is here!"

GOD IS ALWAYS YOUR FATHER!

Who you were before you knew Christ is not who you are now. You belong to God your Father, and He has a master plan for your life! Ephesians 2:10 (NLT) says "For we are God's masterpiece. He has created us anew in Christ Jesus, so we can do the good things He planned for us long ago." Before God ever created Adam and Eve thousands of years ago, He already had planned the good things in store for your life today.

You are no accident or surprise to God! You may not have been planned by your parents, but God your Father planned you before the foundations of the earth were laid! Jeremiah 1:5 (NIV) says, "Before I formed you in the womb I knew you, before you were born I set you apart."

Before time began, you were set apart to do good works for God's kingdom.

God has put His Spirit inside you to help navigate you through this life. You were designed to work toward things God has set in your heart to do. Psalm 34:7 (ESV) says, "Delight yourself in the LORD, and He will give you the desires of your heart." There is no need for interpretation. God means what He said: He wants to meet your every desire in this life!

Here's the key: the closer you come to God, the more your desires become like His. By fulfilling your desires, God is really fulfilling His desires, because you both have the same desires! Hebrews 12:29 (NASB) tells us, "For our God is a consuming fire." When you draw close to God, expect to be warmed. Expect to be set on fire by God!

The apostle Paul encourages the early church in Galatia in Galatians 4:18 (NKJV) when he says, "But it is good to be zealous in a good thing always, and not only when I am present with you." In other words, it is good to be zealous for good works even when you are not at church or around a spiritual leader. Once you have been around God, keep your inner fire for good works going.

Expect God to break out in other people's lives because His fire is always lit within you.

When you experience the fire of God in your spirit, use it. Don't put it out. God wants to spread His kingdom like an all-consuming fire through you!

Daily Reading:
Genesis 1:26-2:3
Ephesians 2:1-10

Thought for the Day:
Have you ever accepted Jesus Christ to come and abide in your heart? What are songs or Bible verses that stir the fire of God in you every time you hear or read them?

Conclusion

T hank you for joining me on this thirty-one day spiritual journey. I hope you have grown closer to God and discovered things in God's word you may not have known were there before! God has an awesome plan for your life. He is always fighting your battles for you. Lamentations 3:23 (NLT) says, "Great is His faithfulness; His mercies begin afresh each morning." Each day you can wake up knowing you have a fresh clean slate with God.

The Lord is excited in what He has planned for your life every day!

Regardless of where you are in life right now, or whatever issues you are facing, I believe God has already stored up blessings and promises He wants to bring to fulfillment. The greater the size of your problems, know that God is even greater. Jeremiah 32:17 (NASB) declares, "Ah Lord God! Behold, You have made the heavens and the earth by Your great power and by Your outstretched arm! Nothing is too difficult for You!"

Instead of magnifying the problem, magnify your God.

Psalm 34:3-4 tells us when we magnify God and praise His name, He will deliver us from all our fears. Fear magnifies problems; faith magnifies God. Take your fears, problems, concerns, and petitions to the Lord. Release your faith by actively reading and learning the Word of God then speaking His word into your life and into the lives of others. Watch the Lord begin to turn your mountain of problems into molehills so you can move forward into the Promised Land of what God has placed in your heart.

Set aside time every day to be alone with God. Build your faith by spending time with Him daily. As you grow in your personal times with the Lord, He will fill your life with His best for you! Isaiah 41:10 (NIV) says, "So do not fear, for I am with you; do not be dismayed, for I am your God. I will strengthen you and help you; I will uphold you with My righteous right hand."

God has promised that no matter what, He is always with you.

God says to acknowledge His presence everywhere you go, and He will show up to do great things. He is with you when you go to work and stays at work until it is time for you to leave. He is with you when you sit in class and grow your knowledge from teachers He has put around you. He is with you when you are raising children to become great leaders for Him. God is always with you.

God says you are His anointed.

The apostle John in 1 John 2:20 describes us as having been anointed by the Holy One. In other words, God has poured out the oil of His goodness to set you apart for His purposes.

One of the greatest mysteries of following Christ is giving up your life to serve Him. Jesus says in Matthew 16:25 (NKJV), "For whoever desires to save his life will lose it, but whoever loses his life for My sake will find it." Jesus' statement sounds as if He is contradicting Himself, but the Lord is actually making an ironic statement about how God's world works.

Conclusion

In God's kingdom, those who give up their right to live their own lives the way they want will actually gain everything God has to give, and those who only live for themselves will lose whatever they could have received from God. I don't know about you, but I want *everything* God has for me!

So, how can you access everything God has for you? The Bible tells us very clearly in John 14:6 (NIV) when Jesus declares, "I am the way and the truth and the life. No one comes to the Father except through Me."

There is only one path to Heaven, and that is through Jesus Christ.

No other name in Heaven or on earth can get you into God's eternal kingdom. Romans 6:23 (NLT) says, "For the wages of sin is death, but the free gift of God is eternal life through Christ Jesus our Lord." Our shortcomings and sins are what separate us from God, who is perfect and holy, but God, already knowing that all of us would mess up at different points in our lives, sent His Son Jesus Christ to die on the cross to redeem us from all sins making us spotless and perfect in His sight!

In other words, because of God's free gift of salvation in Jesus, you are guaranteed to live with Him forever, even after this life. Instead of receiving eternal death for your sins you receive eternal life because you have received Him into your life as your personal Lord and Savior.

Romans 10:9 (NLT) says, "If you confess with your mouth that Jesus is Lord and believe in your heart that God raised Him from the dead, you will be saved." Maybe you have never verbally professed Jesus is the Lord of your life. Or, maybe you have received Christ into your heart in the

past, but you know it is time to rededicate your life to live
for Him. If so, right where you are, open up your heart to
God and say a prayer out loud, something like this:

Lord Jesus,

Come into my heart. I repent of my sins.
Thank you for dying for my sins that I may
live with You forever in eternity.

In Jesus' Name,
Amen.

If you prayed that prayer I believe you have been saved
forever. The Bible says you have been born again to live a
new life for God. Today, you are set free from every chain
of the enemy. I believe even right now that sickness and
disease is leaving, that addictions are permanently being
broken off from your life, and that your joy of new life is
coming out like never before! Nehemiah 8:10 declares that
the joy of the Lord is your strength!

God has created you to be more than a conqueror through
Christ. Have goals. Set dreams into motion by taking steps
as God leads your heart. Read your Bible and pray God's
awesome promises over your life. If you aren't in church,
begin looking for and attending a good Bible-based church
with fellow born-again believers. If you have not been
water baptized by full water immersion, ask a local pastor
to baptize you as a public profession of your faith in Jesus
Christ.

The apostle Paul says that through God's Holy Spirit, He
has gifted you with all sorts of gifts. Romans 12:6-8 (NCV)

says, "We all have different gifts, each of which came because of the grace God gave us. The person who has the gift of prophecy should use that gift in agreement with the faith. Anyone who has the gift of serving should serve. Anyone who has the gift of teaching should teach. Whoever has the gift of encouraging others should encourage. Whoever has the gift of giving to others should give freely. Anyone who has the gift of being a leader should try hard when he leads. Whoever has the gift of showing mercy to others should do so with joy." When you get around other believers, it's like kindling a holy fire for God to draw out all your many spiritual gifts. Being in fellowship with other Christians is crucial to your walk with God!

You have gifts God wants to activate in order to bring change in your life and the lives of others. God has gifted you with so many talents to express His goodness. Whether your talents include teaching, writing, engineering, counseling, ministering, serving, or leading, you are called to use them for God's glory. The apostle Paul encouraged the early church to stay zealous and always keep your inner fire going for good works.

Stay faithful to God and know His breakthroughs of victory in your life are always on the way!

For more information, visit
www.mckademarshall.com

Join me on your favorite social networking sites!

Twitter.com/McKadeMarshall   Facebook.com/McKadeMarshallOfficial

**I am praying for you and believing for God's best in your
life. I'd love to hear from you! To contact me, write to:**

McKade Marshall
PO Box 533
Malibu, California 90265

MLM Publishing

Made in the USA
Monee, IL
15 October 2023

44617013R00089